Effective LEAs and School Improvement

Effective LEAs and School Improvement examines the ways in which local education authorities can support and challenge schools to raise educational standards. The book includes case studies of effective LEAs and interludes from heads and governors on their experience of working with LEAs.

Includes chapters on:

- the role of LEAs in school improvement
- raising standards through the Education Development Plan
- dealing with schools causing concern
- promoting and disseminating good practice
- managing school improvement
- school improvement partnerships
- new model LEAs

Effective LEAs and School Improvement enables local education authorities to learn from existing good practice and to reflect upon their current situation and plan ahead to meet future demands. It is essential reading for all LEAs concerned with raising educational standards.

David Woods is a Senior Educational Advisor for the Standards and Effectiveness Unit at the DfEE and formerly Head of Birmingham LEA's Advisory and Support Service. **Martyn Cribb** is Head of Standards and School Development in Tower Hamlets LEA and formerly a Senior Education Advisor in the DfEE and HMI.

Effective LEAs and School Improvement
Making a Difference

Edited by David Woods and Martyn Cribb

London and New York

First published 2001 by RoutledgeFalmer
11 New Fetter Lane, London EC4P 4EE

Simultaneously published in the USA and Canada
by RoutledgeFalmer
29 West 35th Street, New York, NY 10001

RoutledgeFalmer is an imprint of the Taylor & Francis Group

Typeset in Sabon by Wearset, Boldon, Tyne and Wear
Printed and bound in Great Britain by MPG Books Ltd, Bodmin

British Library Cataloguing in Publication Data
A catalogue record for this book is available from the British Library

Library of Congress Cataloging in Publication Data
Effective LEAS and school improvement : making a difference /
[edited by] David Woods and Martyn Cribb.
   p. cm.
   Includes bibliographical references and index.
      1. School management and organization—Great Britain.
      2. School districts—Great Britain. I. Woods, David, 1942–
      II. Cribb, Martyn.
LB2900.5 .E44 2001
379.1'58'0941—dc21
                                                    00-054291
ISBN 0-415-23265-1 (Hbk)
ISBN 0-415-23266-X (Pbk)

Contents

Figures and tables

Figures

Tables

Contributors

Stella Blackmore is Chief Inspector, Warwickshire LEA.

Tim Brighouse is Chief Education Officer, City of Birmingham.

Patrice Canavan is Headteacher of Sion Manning RC Girls School, Royal Borough of Kensington and Chelsea.

Martyn Cribb is Head of Standards and School Development in Tower Hamlets LEA.

David Maclean is Head of Learning and Achievement, Havering LEA.

Steve Munby is Assistant Director of Education, Blackburn with Darwen Borough Council.

Mark Pattison is Director of Education, Blackburn with Darwen Borough Council.

Diane Simmonds is a Senior Education Adviser, DfEE.

Fran Stevens is Chair of the Birmingham Governors' Forum.

Vanessa Wiseman is Headteacher of Langdon School, Newham LEA.

David Woods is a Senior Education Adviser, DfEE.

Introduction

Local education authorities have been in existence for almost 100 years but in the last ten years in particular there has been a great deal of debate about their functions and future and a rapidly changing policy context. This book looks in particular at effective LEAs and school improvement and examines the ways in which LEAs can make a difference to the raising of educational standards. It draws upon some of the key publications of the Audit Commission related to LEAs: *Losing an Empire, Finding a Role* (1989), *Changing Partners* (1998) and *Held in Trust* (1999); and of the DfEE: *Excellence in Schools* (1997), *Raising Aspirations in the 21st Century* (2000) and *The Role of the Local Education Authority in School Education* (2000); as well as OfSTED and Audit Commission inspection evidence of some 90 (three-fifths) of LEAs to date published in *LEA Support for School Improvement* (February 2001). The Local Government Association and the Education Network (TEN) have also produced a series of booklets on LEA effectiveness on different themes, including *What Makes a Good LEA?* and *Adding Value to School Improvement* (both in 2000). In terms of research the NFER have produced a number of studies over the years, most recently a study of 10 LEAs entitled *The LEA Role in School Improvement* (July 2000), and the Roehampton Institute has assessed the effectiveness of some 20 LEAs since 1996 from the perspective of users (heads, governors and teachers) and providers (officers and councillors), using surveys and interviews. However, relatively little has been published about the work of individual LEAs, although there have been some case studies collected either through the LGA or through the Standards and Effectiveness Unit at the DfEE which have been published on the Standards Site.

This book attempts to redress that balance through examining and illustrating the impact of legislative changes in terms of the LEAs' statutory duty to raise standards and the LEAs' responses to these challenges.

Chapter 1 examines the changing role of LEAs in school improvement with reference to Education Development Plans, the Code of Practice on LEA–School Relations, Fair Funding and the LEA Framework for Inspection and LEAs' relationships with their stakeholders and partners such as heads, teachers, governors, parents and communities.

Chapter 2 examines the support and challenge role of LEAs in school improvement with particular reference to the work of local Inspection and Advisory Services, whilst Chapter 3 looks at the impact of LEA Education Development Plans as the principal instrument for school improvement through audit, establishing priorities, focused action planning, support for underachieving groups, partnerships with schools and other agencies and systematic monitoring and evaluation.

Chapter 4 picks up a vital element of LEAs' powers and duties – to deal with schools causing concern, whether they be designated as being under achieving, having serious weaknesses, or requiring special measures by OfSTED, or likely to fall into such categories if there is no LEA intervention.

Chapter 5 looks at the LEA role in promoting and disseminating good practice and strategies to identify, connect, quality assure, and further develop good practice wherever and whenever it occurs.

From these chapters we get a strong sense of how effective LEAs are at implementing new legislation and rising to the challenge of raising education standards in partnership with central government, whether it be through building better partnerships and capacity, strategic planning, refocusing services or implementing service plans in the context of best value.

The final three chapters of the book are extended case studies of effective LEAs and school improvement taken from three very different types and sizes of LEA – county, metropolitan and unitary. Birmingham, Warwickshire and Blackburn with Darwen have all had very good inspection reports and the latter is a beacon council. The Warwickshire case study looks at strategic professional development for building capacity, raising the quality of teaching, developing leadership and management and promoting self-evaluation and review. The Birmingham case study considers the leadership and management of school improvement and the Blackburn with Darwen case study details a number of frameworks for partnerships to improve urban schooling and implementing key strategies for school improvement.

This is a critical time for LEAs as they seek to restructure, refocus and re-culture their services to meet new and challenging agendas. They stand uncomfortably between the growing assertiveness of central government on the one hand and the principles of successful schools on the other, likely to be criticised from both ends of the spectrum.

Yet they are still well placed to make a difference and to add value to school improvement. They have a statutory duty to promote high standards of education and an important role in school improvement through monitoring the performance of all their schools and especially by helping schools which are identified by OfSTED as under-achieving or giving cause for concern. The LEA also has a role in facilitating collaboration and networking so that good practice is spread more widely. LEAs have already demonstrated in the years their valuable role in implementing many national initiatives such as the National Literacy and Numeracy strategies and the National Grid for Learning as well as working with and through a whole series of partnerships to raise standards in particular the Early Years Development and childcare partnerships, Excellence in Cities and Education Action Zones. LEAs can also make a significant contribution to school and community social inclusion strategies, and help build learning communities and support community activity working with local partners such as health, police and probation services.

It is in this context that LEAs need to position their efforts to raise standards but to do this they must take full account of Best Value, be prepared to learn from the best practice of each other and of public, voluntary and private sector partners and prove they can adapt quickly to change.

1 The role of LEAs in school improvement

David Woods and Martyn Cribb

LEAs face a demanding and rapidly changing environment. The challenges that they have been set present both an opportunity to grasp and a potential threat to their existence. Expectations of them are clearer than ever before, and LEAs need to devote considerable energy and thought to their key processes of policy and direction, resource management and performance review if they are to meet the challenge.

(*Held in Trust*, Audit Commission 1999)

Changing legislation

Local education authorities were created by the Balfour Education Act of 1902 and until the Education Reform Act of 1988 they were responsible for almost all educational services. The 1988 Act altered their powers significantly. Schools were to offer open enrolment, parents were to be offered real choice in terms of the schools available for their children, a National Curriculum was to be taught and most schools were to be managed through a system of delegated budgeting (LMS), although there were mandatory and discretionary exceptions.

In their report, *Losing an Empire, Finding a Role* (1989), the Audit Commission argued that the LEAs still had significant influence if it exercised this in partnerships with government, schools, parents and communities. In a perceptive passage the report identified six 'rewarding' roles for 'new' LEAs:

- a leader – articulating the vision of what the education service was trying to achieve;
- a partner – supporting schools and colleges;
- a planner – of facilities for the future;
- a provider of information – helping people making informed choices;
- a regulator – the quality assurance function;
- a banker – channelling the funds.

Some LEAs began to adopt this model and forge new relationships with their educational communities. However, successive Education Acts in the

1990s have ensured that the role and function of LEAs, particularly their role in school improvement, has been held up to continuous scrutiny. The 1992 Act further diminished the role of LEAs by removing their power to inspect and setting up the Office for Standards in Education, taking away a significant amount of the Rate Support Grant that paid for inspection and advisory services and allowing the establishment of grant-maintained Schools completely independent of LEAs. The 1997 Act made provision for the inspection of LEAs by HMCI assisted by the Audit Commission. However, the new Labour Government in the White Paper *Excellence in Schools* (1997) set out the comprehensive role LEAs should play in raising standards of achievement, and stated that: 'The LEAs' task is to challenge schools to raise standards continuously and to apply pressure when they do not.' The LEA role in school improvement in relation to individual schools was to:

- challenge schools to raise standards and act as a voice for parents;
- provide clear performance data that can readily be used by schools;
- offer educational services to schools that choose to use them;
- provide focused support to schools that are underperforming;
- focus their efforts on national priorities such as literacy and numeracy; and
- work with the DfEE and other LEAs to help celebrate excellence and to spread best practice.

Excellence in Schools (1997) expressed the hope that this new constructive role 'will replace the uncertainty from which LEAs have suffered in recent years. In return, LEAs will have to be fully accountable. They must demonstrate to their own schools, to parents and the local electorate and to the DfEE that they are doing a good job in improving their schools'. Failure to do this would result in direct government intervention.

Yet as the Audit Commission pointed out in *Changing Partners* (1998), LEAs would have to continue to work in a framework where two fundamental tensions exist:

1   The tension between school autonomy and external intervention. LEAs are expected to intervene where schools are experiencing problems whilst respecting the principle that the main responsibility for raising standards lies with schools themselves.
2   The tension between local and national interests – making policies and decisions at local level and reflecting the legitimate interests of central government.

Moving on from the role outlined in *Losing an Empire, Finding a Role*, *Changing Partners* (1998) (also written by the Audit Commission) suggested four main components of the role of LEAs:

- articulating a vision with a supporting strategy for ensuring high-quality education;
- acting as a vehicle and standards for improvement in standards basing progress on a process of continuous improvement;
- ensuring equity – and an inclusive system of education in local schools; and
- managing trade-offs – balancing the interests of schools, pupils, parents and communities.

Changing Partners stressed the importance of strategic management, developing a coherent set of management processes and creating a high-trust culture so that the effective LEA would:

- meet agreed national and local targets;
- experience standards of achievement that are 'excellent', 'improving', or both;
- achieve the highest effectiveness for the lowest cost; and
- emerge favourably from comparisons with similar LEAs.

With the passing of the School Standards and Framework Act (1998) to add to other legislation, a new 'job description' for LEAs emerged based on four major pillars:

- The LEA Education Development Plan
- The Code of Practice on LEA–School Relations
- Fair Funding
- The LEA Framework for Inspection

'Taken together these four developments constitute the Government's dual strategy of pressure and support, which applies as much to LEAs as it does to schools' (Simon Bird in *The Government Inspectors Call*, TEN, 1999).

The School Standards and Framework Act gave LEAs a new duty, in carrying out all relevant functions, to promote high standards, which applies to education for all those of compulsory school age, whether at school or otherwise, and those above or below that age who are registered as pupils of schools maintained by the authority. As part of that duty every LEA has had to prepare an **Education Development Plan** (EDP) describing the authority's proposals for raising the standards of education and for improving the performance of schools over a three-year period. The EDP is the means by which the LEA articulates its strategy for promoting school improvement and raising standards in all maintained schools and its part in delivering the national priorities for school improvement – literacy and numeracy, schools causing concern, underperforming groups of pupils, SEN including gifted and talented, school self-evaluation, ICT, attendance and behaviour, and disseminating good practice. As such it is the key mechanism for LEAs to meet their statutory duty to raise standards whilst accepting that the primary responsibility for improving standards lies with schools themselves. It has two parts, both required by law: A statement of proposals which includes all the attainment and social exclusion targets for the LEA and a School Improvement Programme setting out the main priorities for improvement and the pattern of activities. LEAs consult with schools and other partners in order that all stakeholders should understand and accept the part they have to play in achieving the plan. The first EDPs were approved to start in April 1999 for a three-year period, subject to general conditions related to annual target setting. The subject of raising standards through the Education Development Plan is covered in depth in Chapter 3.

The **Code of Practice on LEA–School Relations** (DfEE, newly revised in 2000) sets out the principles which should underpin the relationships between LEAs and schools, explains how the role of the LEA in supporting schools is expected to work in practice, and provides guidance on the exercise of those LEA powers and responsibilities which are most relevant to raising standards (particularly with reference to schools causing concern). However, as the Code explains (pp. 10–11),

> Effective Leadership does not rely solely on legal powers. As the best LEAs are already demonstrating, it is as least as much about developing through partnership a culture in which schools want to work with the LEA because they have a shared view with the LEA of the way in which schools should develop for the benefit of their community, they respect and trust the LEAs judgments even when their own performance is being challenged, and they value the many ways in which the LEA can support them in doing better.

The principles of a constructive relationship are maintained in the Revised Code published in February 2001 and what emerges quite strongly is that all LEAs and schools should have raising standards as their overriding aim.

> The highest priority for the Local Education Authority is to promote high standards of education. Key to this is its support for self-improvement in all schools. It needs to monitor information about all schools, and facilitate the sharing of best practice amongst local schools and more widely.

Chapter 2 considers further the characteristics of an effective school improvement service in challenging and supporting schools to raise standards of achievement.

Fair Funding is a revised and extended framework of Local Management of Schools which sets out the LEAs responsibilities in respect of delegated funding to schools and is based on seven principles:

- raising standards in schools;
- self-management for schools;
- clear accountability of both LEA and the school;
- transparency of school finances;
- opportunity for greater responsibility in schools;
- equity between the new categories of schools; and
- value for money for schools and LEA.

LEAs can only retain funds centrally to support their role in relation to schools in four key areas:

- school improvement
- access
- special educational provision
- strategic management.

The category of 'school improvement' includes the preparation and implementation of the EDP, negotiating targets with schools, monitoring the performance of all schools and tackling schools causing concern.

However, funding the LEAs is increasingly targeted through the Standards Fund, often in a matched basis to LEA funds and the management of the Standards fund is crucial to school improvement. Recently the *Modernising Local Government Finance* Green Paper for Education proposed further changes in the funding of local councils' education functions seeking to achieve 90 per cent delegation to schools by no later than 2002–3.

The fourth part of the LEA 'job description' is described in the **LEA Framework for Inspection** (1999), which reviews the way LEAs perform their functions and in particular determines the contributions made by LEAs to school improvement and to high standards of achievement.

Each inspection seeks to answer the following connected questions:

- Does the LEA manage its functions efficiently and economically?
- Does the LEA exercise its functions effectively and in such a way as to promote high standards by improving the quality of education in schools and the achievement of all pupils?
- Does the LEA exercise its functions effectively to ensure that the pupils in its schools are not harmed and, in particular, that action is taken to prevent and address racism and to assist other statutory bodies charged with the protection of children?
- Does the LEA comply with its legal obligations, including equal

opportunities and, in its work, does it have regard to the Code of Practice on LEA–School Relations?

The Audit Commission Survey as part of the LEA inspection process asks schools their views on the LEA strategy and on services the LEA provides to schools. One category relates specifically to the LEA approach to school improvement with reference to the following criteria:

- the clarity of the LEA strategy on school improvement;
- consultation with schools on the EDP;
- the relevance of the LEA's priorities;
- the usefulness of the LEA's monitoring of the school's work;
- support for schools in special measures or having serious weaknesses;
- provision of data on pupil performance and guidance on its use;
- the steps taken to disseminate good practice; and
- the LEA's ability to pursue its priorities.

before going on to ask specific questions about support for improvement in the quality of education and management of schools including the LEA's support for teaching.

Reviewing all the changes made, the Audit Commission in its publication *Held in Trust* (1999) looked again at the role and functions of LEAs, stressing the context of a government placing the raising of educational attainment at the heart of its educational policy. Already targets to raise pupil attainment at Key Stage 2 and Key Stage 4 had been established and a number of key initiatives had been set up to support through the Standards Fund the process of school improvement in particular the development of the National Literacy Strategy, the National Numeracy Strategy and the National Grid for Learning.

The LEA role in promoting school improvement was now at the forefront of its duties. 'Against this background the Government has made it clear that an LEA's success will be judged largely in terms of the educational performance of its schools – school improvement is therefore central to the future of LEAs' (Audit Commission, 1999). This was defined as a responsibility to:

- prepare and implement an EDP;
- negotiate targets with schools;
- monitor the performance of schools; and
- intervene in inverse proportion to success.

However, given that the prime responsibility for school improvement lies with schools themselves, disentangling the impact of LEA support and intervention on the quality of education provided by schools is not easy. Some commentators and heads believe that the impact of LEAs on school improvement is too remote and indistinct to establish a connection whilst others provide case studies of the successful interaction between LEAs and schools in raising standards. However, there does appear to be a general agreement, backed by OfSTED inspection evidence that they can make a positive contribution in particular to:

- the provision and use of performance data;
- support for literacy and numeracy;
- school governance; and
- support for schools in serious weaknesses and special measures.

Clearly, those LEAs with richer data on school performance that can be produced by central government can provide a comprehensive performance framework for their schools, including comparative and trend analysis, information about the performance of a range of pupil groups, individual pupil data sets, that can better inform the choice of priorities. All this data will also provide the basis for targeting LEA intervention according to the needs of schools as well as enabling the LEA to engage in a meaningful dialogue with schools with reference to target setting which is central to school improvement as it aids diagnosis and focuses efforts. LEA Education Development Plans themselves contain statements on the use of data and target setting processes, as well as support for national school improvement priorities such as literacy and numeracy and a strategic statement for dealing with schools causing concern. The effectiveness of LEAs in dealing with such schools can partly be quantified through a study of the number of schools in serious weaknesses and special measures, the statistical trends, and the average time it takes for these schools to escape these categories. What is much more difficult to quantify is the success of the LEA's 'preventative' strategies in making sure that very few schools fall into these categories in the first place.

Whatever the debate about the nature and extent of the LEA's impact on school standards effective LEAs will have a comprehensive understanding of the relative needs of their schools and be able to target support and intervention. A very systematic approach is crucial to the LEA's success whether in identifying priorities or implementing them: 'An effective LEA should know what it is trying to achieve, how it will achieve it and have a set of measures to assess its progress towards the goals' (*Held in Trust*, Audit Commission, 1999: 70)

One further important contextual element in judging effective LEAs and school improvement as well as other functions is the requirement from April 2000 on all local authorities, including LEAs, to obtain best value. This duty requires local authorities to demonstrate:

- that they are delivering services of high quality and effectiveness whilst continually improving performance;

- effective and accountable stakeholder involvement and consultation; and
- a willingness to consider and use alternative methods of service delivery to deliver desired outcomes.

'The continuation of Education Development Plans, Fair Funding and OfSTED LEA inspections provide a comprehensive system for ensuring that LEAs promote high standards in schools and contribute to the Best value process for local government as a whole' (Audit Commission, 1999).

In many cases LEAs are preparing a best-value analysis for the whole of the education department and individual services and are beginning to benchmark the various services of the LEA against similar services elsewhere.

Inspection evidence

In the report of the Senior Chief Inspector for 1998–9 it was stated that there is 'no tradition of at a local level of LEA inspectors inspecting and reporting without fear or favour. Many LEA advisory services, which are now being transmuted into inspectorates, were established to develop and encourage particular approaches and methodologies, not to say philosophies of education'. Many will mourn the passing of the era when the LEAs such as the West Riding of Yorkshire, Oxfordshire, Hertfordshire and ILEA were developing identifiable approaches to the education of children. In some part, the education of the pupils was the result of some outstanding work which had a profound impact on the quality of education received by many pupils. But too much of the work was disjointed and failed to ensure that all pupils received their entitlement to high-quality education.

The inspection of LEAs was begun in a systematic way with the Education Act of 1997. Section 38 of the Act gave the permission for the inspection of 'any function which relates to the provision of education for (a) persons of compulsory school age (whether at school or otherwise) or (b) for persons of any age above or below that age who are registered as pupils at the schools maintained by the authority'. This wide-ranging power set the scene for the detailed examination of the functions of the LEA and the impact which they are having on pupils' standards of achievement.

That LEAs are more accountable in a rigorous and more public way must be a good thing. There is the democratic process of accountability and the Members of each council have a vital role to play in the development of key strategies for the LEA. The role of members in representing the views, aspirations and needs of local people is vital if the education system in an LEA is to take account of their educational requirements. However, the democratic process can lack the rigour and sharp focus of the inspection process.

The inspections of LEAs are especially concerned with the efforts to raise standards and focus on aspects of school improvement. 'The aim of inspection is to review and report on the way LEAs perform their functions and, in particular, to determine the contributions LEAs support, including support to individual pupils, to school improvements and to high standards of achievement' (*LEA Support for School Improvement*, OfSTED, 1999).

LEA inspections are jointly run by OfSTED and the Audit Commission. The broad split of responsibilities appears to be along the lines of OfSTED looking at the school standards issues and the commission looking at the issues of value for money and the strategic management of funds in the LEA. This split appears to work reasonably well and it enables the various professionals to focus on their particular skill areas. Some of the inspections are supplemented by Attached Inspectors who are brought in to supplement the teams.

What has been found?

In HMCI report for 1998-9 it is stated that, although these do not represent a balanced sample, the overall performance of the LEAs is too variable. The report goes on to detail the unacceptably wide variation in the performance of the LEAs. This ranged from LEAs where many of the services were said to be weak or worse (two out of five were said to have serious deficiencies), to LEAs with a balance of strengths and weaknesses through to those described as having many strengths. In June 2000, OfSTED published a Draft Paper for Consultation entitled *LEA Support for School Improvement*, which analysed the first 44 inspection reports ending in September 1999, with some reference to inspections carried out in the autumn term of 1999. As the report accepts, these were not necessarily representative of LEAs as a whole. It found that over the three years of inspection there had been signs of improvement in LEA performance albeit from a low base, although two-fifths of LEAs had more weaknesses than strengths. However, there was a growing polarisation between the best run LEAs and those that had more weaknesses than strengths. Nevertheless, the report stated that 'the inspections suggests that LEAs can, and often do, contribute effectively to aspects of improvement in individual schools', but on the central question of whether LEAs can lead to a rapid rise in overall standards they entered a verdict of 'not proven'. HMCI's latest report (1999–2000) states that there has been intervention in 18 LEAs. 'The success of the intervention cannot yet be judged, because the seven re-inspections conducted during the year were exclusively of LEAs .... In which intervention had not occurred. In three of the LEAs – Tower Hamlets, Barnsley and Manchester – the great improvements were due to:

• effective leadership from the Director of Education;

- political support at the local level;
- a determination to address rigorously the recommendations of the original report.

The OfSTED and Audit Commission report on 'Local Education Authority Support for School Improvement (February 2001) is equivocal in its support for LEAs. On the one hand it states that 'some LEAs ... are impressive organisations ...' and lists the many strong characteristics including having 'viable strategies to enhance schools' own capacity to sustain continuous improvement. Presumably these strategies work but a little later in the report in paragraph 16 the report's authors question whether LEAs make a difference. Further the report states that 'The relationship between the effectiveness of LEA support and school standards are not consistent or very clear'.

An analysis of inspection evidence by Barber and Turner in *Recognising LEA Effectiveness* found that LEAs were deficient in:

- not understanding and effectively implementing the notion of support and challenge;
- not targeting effectively support and challenge in inverse proportion to success;
- the management of advisory services;
- performance management systems and induction for LEA advisers; and
- providing appropriate support for secondary schools.

However, they found a number of areas of strength:

- use of performance data to help schools set targets and with self-evaluation;
- support for schools with special measures;
- literacy and numeracy;
- support for ethnic minority pupils;
- support for individual pupils with special educational needs;
- financial, legal, payroll and personnel support services.

A further analysis of a sample of the latest inspection reports using some of the key functions of the LEA as a heading shows the following:

- most LEAs have a clear vision for education and this is usually shared by schools and other stakeholders;
- improvement in standards of achievement are highest in LEAs where the strategic management is strong;
- inspection and advice to schools is variable, is best in primary schools and weakest in secondary schools;

- support for schools causing concern was varied – for schools subject to special measures it is generally sound, for schools with serious weaknesses it is weak in about one third of cases;
- use of performance data to assist schools set targets and raise standards is usually sound and in many cases good;
- support for special educational needs is variable and LEAs face the problem of trying to satisfy schools and parents in the face of limited resources;
- LEA support for ethnic minority achievement varied from good to unsatisfactory with some LEAs having significant internal variations;
- provision of budget information is usually timely and in only a minority of cases was it regarded as a significant weakness; and
- information and communication technology is a weakness in a number of LEAs.

Overall, the quality of the LEAs' Inspection and Advisory Services, which are central to the drive to raise standards, is judged as being particularly variable and deficient in those LEAs which are not having a direct impact on the pupils' standards of achievement. In some cases it appears that although the LEA is doing well overall there is insufficient emphasis and quality of support for the schools. However, recent LEA inspection evidence shows that LEAs have improved considerably in carrying out the functions of challenge, support, intervention and monitoring. Five London LEAs are reported to demonstrate particular good practice, with the following features:

- clear definition of the respective functions of schools and LEA, with adequate resourcing;
- close, but not cosy, relationships with schools accepting that the LEA had the right to challenge them;
- high calibre staff, usually link advisers or inspectors, who had credibility with schools and were able to provide, not only rigorous evaluation, but also strategies for improvement;
- a preparedness to take on complacent schools;
- detailed knowledge of schools . . .;
- effective targeting of the work of the service . . . LEA Support for School Improvement P.20

The latest HMCI report states that in about half the LEAs inspected there were weaknesses in the capacity of some advisers to challenge schools in any meaningful way. This is sometimes due to the poor quality of relationships while in others it is due to the lack of experience or expertise of the advisers. This highlights an important weakness in the current state of training for LEA advisers and inspectors. There are two aspects which need to be considered. In the first place few LEAs would deny that it is important that advisers go through the OfSTED training for inspector status. This was appropriate in the early days when OfSTED was actively recruiting inspectors but currently it is very difficult for the LEA advisers or anybody else to gain accreditation. OfSTED claims that there are sufficient inspectors and there is no need to train any more but if there remains a need for the LEA advisers to be trained and to participate in the activities of inspection. Second, there is a lack of training for LEA advisers in the skills required to turn round schools. There is no doubt that LEA advisory teams benefit from the knowledge and experience brought by the experienced head-teachers in this regard but all advisers benefit from proper induction and training in the role of support and challenge to schools and in particular dealing with schools causing concern. Consultants or seconded heads add value to the service but many of them need to adjust to the role as they miss the hands on management and the ability to make things happen. Advisory work is about challenging and supporting and not necessarily doing the job for the headteachers. It is about building capacity and leaving the schools better placed to do the job than they were before the advisers arrived.

However, as the DfEE's policy paper on *The Role of the LEA in School Education* (2000) points out, the lack of established professional standards for the key school improvement functions of monitoring, challenge and intervention make it hard for authorities to know under best value criteria whether their own services are up to scratch, and equally important whether alternative providers are of a high enough standard. The paper goes on to propose a system of national recognition of school improvement services which would apply common professional and business standards to cover LEA in-house provision and voluntary sector alternatives being developed. The best advisory and inspection services are able to balance very successfully the concepts of monitoring, intervention, challenge and support, although as the NFER report on *The LEA Contribution to School Improvement* (July 2000) points out, 'it requires a remarkable level of professional skill to fulfil the expectations required of a critical friend, professional adviser, inspector, ally, change agent, and bearer of challenging messages'. The new national professional standards should improve quality across the service.

During the last few years advisory and inspection services have been reduced in size mainly due to less funding being retained centrally by LEAs, although many of these services have proved their worth by being bought back by schools. However, the requirements for EDPs and other support plans, and the need to implement national school improvement initiatives have made even greater demands on this resource. This clearly reinforces the need for LEAs to get the absolute best out of these services through being very clear about the core agenda and the support services to be provided whilst precisely targeting support and intervention. The role of Advisory and Inspection Services is explored in depth in Chapter 2.

A key feature of good LEAs emerging from the OfSTED evidence is a shared vision and purpose that binds together schools, officers, members and LEA partners in a determination to drive up standards and achieve excellence. Such LEAs have a clear set of objectives which reflect corporate and national priorities and share the following characteristics in their support for school improvement:

- communication and consultation with stakeholders;
- a rigorous and responsive management system with the capacity to be innovative and challenging;
- services to schools that represent best value for money;
- a capacity to intervene quickly to ensure that schools do not slip into failure;
- the drive to deal with and eradicate failure;
- forging new partnerships to secure school improvement; and
- the continual reinforcement of success and the celebration of achievement.

New developments

Recently (October 2000) the DfEE have produced a policy paper on *The Role of the LEA in School Education* which seeks to provide a clear vision of the LEA's roles and how it can most effectively be discharged. It needs to be read in connection with the revised *Code of Practice on LEA–School Relations* (2000) and with the Green Paper on *Modernising Local Government Finance*, (2000) which deals with the funding of local councils' education functions.

The role of the LEA in relation to schools is summarised under five headings – special educational needs, access, school improvement and tackling failure, educating excluded pupils, pupil welfare and strategic management. Under 'School improvement and tackling failure', the role is summed up as:

- monitoring the performance of all schools and ensuring they have the necessary information to set and meet demanding targets for all groups of pupils;
- focusing their school improvement services on schools which need challenge and further support to secure improvement . . . and intervening decisively where a school is failing its pupils; and
- drawing together Education Authority and school targets and the Authority's contribution to meeting them in an Education Developmental Plan.

The second part of the paper 'modernising methods of working' includes sections on new ways of working which includes a more open market in school services as well as sharing school improvement responsibilities with groups of schools. It also covers new ways of discharging responsibilities in partnership and national professional standards and recognition for school improvement services.

The paper concludes by saying

> We are therefore establishing a clear and firm base which the Education Authority of the future can develop. We will welcome widespread debate on how we can ensure that all support services, local or national, aid the task of raising standards, improving quality of delivery and securing fairness in the use and outcome of public investment in the education system.

The following chapters should be read in the context of this changing policy.

2   Challenge and support to schools

David Maclean

> What emerged overall was that the challenge aspect of the role was more acceptable to both headteachers and advisers, and less likely to damage the relationship if it was grounded in a positive working relationship and channelled in an open but non-confrontational manner.
>
> (*The LEA Contribution to School Improvement*, NFER, 2000: 34)

The purpose of this chapter is to give consideration to the characteristics of an effective school-improvement service in challenging and supporting schools to build their capacity to raise standards of achievement. Until relatively recently, there has been very little exploration of how effective LEA services can add value to school improvement. This, in part, has been due to:

- the focus on how well schools perform – including the research base on school effectiveness and school improvement;
- the lack of clarity about the role of the LEA in school improvement; and
- the difficulty of establishing a causal link between LEA input and pupil performance outputs.

However, this has significantly changed due to current legislation which puts pressure on local authorities to demonstrate:

- how they provide leadership and secure commitment from teachers, headteachers and governors to the local vision and direction of the service;
- how they provide support and challenge in monitoring school progress;
- how they identify, promote and celebrate best practice in schools; and
- how they have systems and procedures to enable them to intervene in inverse proportion to need.

Moreover, the inspection of LEAs, the requirement for best value reviews and the provision of LEA performance data through the OfSTED

ance and Assessment (PANDA) has placed much of the relevant
the public domain.

A successful LEA: some features

Leadership is recognised for developing a culture of high expectations and achievement. There is commitment from all stakeholders to the vision, which is constantly reaffirmed through the language, symbols and signs of all senior staff in schools and in the Education Department. Relationships between officers, advisers and headteachers are based on professional dialogue. Effective challenge, mutual understanding and respect for each other's roles and responsibilities and the collective will to listen, collate, learn and move forward are key features. All key policy areas and procedures for working with schools are developed in partnership and are totally transparent. There is a culture of celebration, based on the knowledge of all schools, which enables families of schools and practitioners to learn from the best. Senior managers in both schools and the directorate are seen as experts, each responsible for the overall goal but also assisting each other to deliver with flexible opportunities to move in and out of role through shadowing, monitoring progress, mentoring, leading teams and initiatives. In all this, there is an appetite to base judgements on evidence, to learn from both success and failure and to lead by example. There is an expectation that once all priorities and plans have been put in place, there will be rigorous self-review to demonstrate and celebrate what has been achieved. The team of advisers is close-knit, highly credible, very visible and, through a shared set of values, code of conduct and set of quality standards, highly confident in all that they do.

Advisers working in an effective LEA are known not only by headteachers, but also by governors, teachers and members for the leadership role they take and the impact they have on the school improvement agenda.

A key set indicators for an effective Advisory Inspection Service (AIS) would include descriptors and impact measures for each of the following areas:

- ensuring and gaining commitment to the vision;
- providing challenge and support based on the analysis of both performance data and local intelligence;
- providing strategic support to raising standards in
  - literacy, numeracy and ICT
  - leadership and management
  - underachieving groups;
- promoting and supporting diversification, innovation and social inclusion; and
- ensuring service quality assurance and best value.

A descriptor for effective challenge and support

To ensure challenge and support, an effective AIS will have the following characteristics:

- leading a well co-ordinated, cross-departmental approach to develop a coherent profile of each school;
- systematic programmes of school visits undertaken by link adviser/inspector or LEA team;
- rationale for the visits programme shared with headteachers and governors in terms of
  - the timing of each visit
  - themes to be monitored
  - purposes of the monitoring programme;
- clear accountabilities and expectations for advisers and opportunities for headteacher feedback;
- an annual school-improvement calendar, with clear objectives and LEA links to the EDP;
- ensuring differentiated, additional support is
  - co-ordinated across appropriate services
  - treated as a priority
  - led by a senior officer reporting outcomes to senior management team;
- ensuring governors have clear understanding of their school's performance; and
- deciding upon appropriate levels of support and challenge to ensure that all schools have effective and rigorous approaches to school self-review.

The use and communication of performance data

Without doubt, one of the most significant changes to have taken place in the education service is the importance now attached to performance data. This applies at national, local, school and, most crucially, pupil level. The collection, analysis and interpretation of performance data is now integral to improvement planning. Both schools and authorities have made significant progress in:

- developing appropriate management information systems;
- implementing value-added approaches;
- developing guidance and training on target setting, linked to the performance of individual pupils;
- benchmarking performance in comparison to families of schools and LEAs; and
- setting and monitoring challenging targets for improvement.

To a degree the volume and type of data now available to both schools and LEAs can be daunting, and there are issues about:

- the amount of data;
- the timing and availability of data;
- the repetition of data; and
- training and support for governors and headteachers.

At best, data is a powerful tool to assist in school self-review and priority setting. At worst it can cause information overload and confusion.

In developing approaches to working with schools on performance data, effective LEAs:

- provide analyses which complement analyses received through the DfEE's Autumn Package and OfSTED PANDA by adding local comparators;
- develop a common language and understanding in data use and analysis;
- work towards the notion of a pupil 'entitlement to progress';
- encourage and facilitate the development of families of similar schools to learn from emerging and best practice; and
- provide tools to enable interrogation and diagnosis.

In addition, the analysis of performance data has been used to identify groupings of schools and more importantly, triggers, where schools appear to be vulnerable or at risk. Such triggers typically are cross-directorate and include:

- capacity issues   – schools with high percentage of surplus places
                        – localities of significant mismatch
- behaviour issues   – schools with greatest numbers of exclusions
                        – schools with lowest attendance rates
- financial issues   – schools with carry forward higher than 5 per cent
                        – schools with significant deficit budgets
- SEN issues   – school mismatch between predicted and actual numbers on stages
                        – school mismatch between spend and need
- staffing issues   – staff turnover and vacancy rates
                        – sickness rates
- achievement issues – lower quartile of achievement
                        – low achievement of specific groups
                        – sharp decline in standards.

The following are examples of LEA practice, which highlight the ways advisory and inspection services, working with research and information services, can provide leadership and support in the use of performance data.

Case study 1: Essex LEA

In one LEA, advisers have developed software to analyse Key Stage 1 and 2 mathematics and science results to help teachers use this assessment data to diagnostically inform teacher planning. Using the software, it is possible to identify which questions children have not answered correctly, identify trends within classes, diagnose areas of maths and science in which children seem to have misconceptions and identify those areas where further teaching is needed. The template below provides the framework for this analysis. Teachers are invited to forward their analysis to the Advisory and Inspection Service (AIS), enabling county-wide trends to be identified, which then inform the programme of in-service education and training (INSET) and school consultancy. Published aggregate data is published to all county schools in the *Science News*.

Case study 2: Suffolk LEA

This example shows how an LEA provides the following data annually to headteachers in primary schools to help them identify underachieving pupils:

- Baseline, KS1 and 2 National Curriculum tests, standardised reading and mathematics test data and analysis of each, including county and national comparators for 7, 9 and 11-year-olds;
- value-added progress charts and tables for 9 and 11-year-olds, including individual pupils residuals;
- an individual school profile summarising and comparing test and school value-added performance for a range of indicators over a three-year period;
- local benchmark groups of schools for KS1 and KS2; and
- school data management software – a system produced by the LEA in consultation with schools to track and analyse individual pupil performance using data collected and distributed electronically as pupils move school.

Officers use the full range of data available for independent analysis. In particular, the data is used:

- to indicate the appropriate range in which a school would be expected to set its targets;
- to identify triggers in identifying vulnerable or at risk schools;
- by advisers in preparation for the visit programme to review progress and inform the target-setting process; and
- to benchmark the LEA's performance against other LEAs.

Core programme of visits

Whilst the analysis of performance data provides an objective audit of how schools are performing, effective LEAs balance such analysis with systematic programmes of school visits. The combination of these two approaches enables the LEA to know its schools – both in terms of strengths and weaknesses. The dilemma, however, is how to ensure the best deployment of limited resources whilst ensuring the LEA knows all of its schools. The advisory and inspection service is key to fulfilling this role, but increasingly in collaboration with special needs and pupil support services. Most authorities now have planned, systematic programmes of visits, linking school monitoring to the priorities and action plans set out in the LEA Education Development Plan.

This, of course, has not always been the case. In the 'pre-trading' era, teams were characterised by considerable variation in expertise and inconsistency of practice and message. The cult of the individual was rife. At a time prior to extensive LMS, many advisers had considerable control over appointments, curricular direction, deployment of their resources, including advisory teachers, but most importantly, control over their diaries. With the onset of trading, AIS had rapidly to come to terms with market testing, focus groups, repositioning the service, financial transparency and trading capacity. Most recently, the school improvement era has highlighted the AIS core business, translated nationally through EDPs and associated action plans. In addition, the *Code of Practice on LEA–School Relations* provides a further challenge to advisory and inspection services in how they deliver their role. Clarity in the role of the AIS about meeting the school improvement agenda is helpful in portraying school/LEA relations in terms of a constructive partnership in which there is mutual recognition of the functions and contributions of each party. Significantly, the Code states the following:

> A wide range of local authority and LEA staff have contact with schools. But LEA advisory staff have a particular part to play in relation to school performance and the standards of teaching and learning – helping schools to analyse their current standards and the factors which influence them, and to identify effective ways of improving; helping schools to keep in touch with good and developing practice; and working with schools on target setting and action planning.
>
> (paragraph 72)

and in addition:

> The LEA has a central role in managing and supporting the implementation of the National Literacy and Numeracy Strategies in primary schools. In addition to agreeing targets with each school, this includes providing training for all schools and ensuring there are appropriate mechanisms for monitoring their progress and providing support where required.
>
> (paragraph 76)

Table 2.1 Changes in approaches to advisory work

From	To
interests of headteacher and school	interests of learner and pupil advocacy
performance descriptors with focus on process	measures of impact with focus on standards
low-level individual accountability	high level individual accountability
'my schools'	'schools I challenge and support'
'my diary'	allocation of target days
being wide ranging	focus on core business

A core programme of AIS visits must, therefore:

- meet the requirements of the Code of Practice;
- conform to the resource limitations identified in the *EDP Guidance* to LEAs from the DfEE (September, 1998);
- be transparent and agreed with schools;
- be well planned, managed and recorded;
- be supported by effective staff development;
- meet the need to challenge, support, celebrate and, where necessary, intervene; and
- be cyclical in nature.

A typical programme might look like the one shown in Table 2.2.

The details of each term's work will vary with the stage of development in relation to the LEA's EDP priorities. An example of a proforma developed to support the collection of data to monitor the first theme set out in this visit programme is shown in Table 2.3.

In addition to the core programme of visits more intense support is provided to schools in varying degrees of vulnerability, risk, serious weakness and special measures as indicated in Figure 2.2. In meeting this challenge, effective LEAs have moved quickly to find ways of auditing and identifying need, developing classifications of schools based on standards and performance and ensuring that schools can engage effectively with the process. Systems for classifying schools will need to be based on judgements about standards, judgements about trends and, most difficult, judgements about a school's capacity to improve. These aspects are further developed in Chapter 3.

Table 2.2 A typical programme of AIS visits

(1) Analysis of data and target setting	*Autumn term*

Interrogation and interpretation of data (PANDA, OfSTED, SATs,
　GCSE, school data)
Benchmarking against other schools
Develop school profile based on EQF
Analysing information from performance data and agreeing targets
Monitoring progress towards previous targets
Helping senior managers to analyse and act upon performance data
Challenging senior managers in the target-setting process
Agreeing with headteacher and chair of governors the outcomes
　of this process

(2) School-based strategic planning	*Spring term*

Review the appropriateness of the school improvement plan
Check success criteria in relation to key issues for improvement
Evaluate the quality of the plan and the likely impact on attainment
　with reference to the relevant diversions of EQF
Work with senior managers and/or curriculum leaders on
　improvement planning
Review plan in relation to key issues and school performance tables

(3) Monitoring and evaluation	*Summer term*

Evaluate with schools their self-review processes (see Figure 2.1)
Monitor progress on post-OfSTED action plan
Update school profile
Identify examples of best practice
Assist the school gather evidence of progress in implementing the
　key issues arising from its improvement plan and OfSTED
　action plan
Further develop self-review systems using the Essex Quality
　Framework (EQF)
Further develop the skills of staff and governors in monitoring
　and evaluation
Provide feedback on progress to senior managers and to the LEA.

Source: Essex LEA

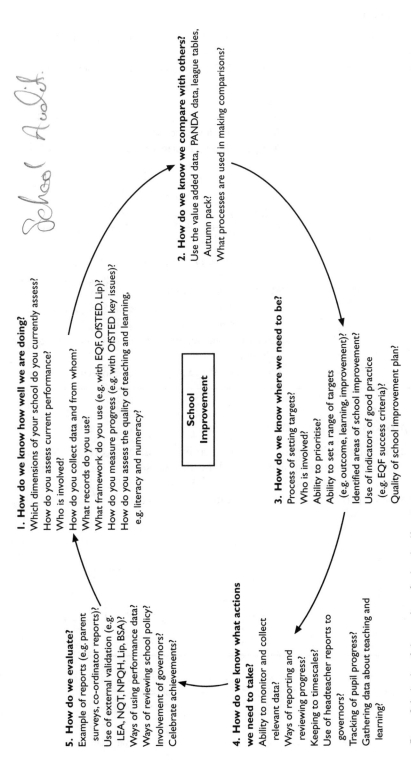

School Audit.

1. How do we know how well we are doing?
Which dimensions of your school do you currently assess?
How do you assess current performance?
Who is involved?

How do you collect data and from whom?
What records do you use?
What framework do you use (e.g. with EQF, OfSTED, Lip)?
How do you measure progress (e.g. with OfSTED key issues)?
How do you assess the quality of teaching and learning,
e.g. literacy and numeracy?

2. How do we know we compare with others?
Use the value added data, PANDA data, league tables,
Autumn pack?
What processes are used in making comparisons?

School
Improvement

3. How do we know where we need to be?
Process of setting targets?
Who is involved?
Ability to prioritise?
Ability to set a range of targets
(e.g. outcome, learning, improvement)?
Identified areas of school improvement?
Use of indicators of good practice
(e.g. EQF success criteria)?
Quality of school improvement plan?

**4. How do we know what actions
we need to take?**
Ability to monitor and collect
relevant data?
Ways of reporting and
reviewing progress?
Keeping to timescales?
Use of headteacher reports to
governors?
Tracking of pupil progress?
Gathering data about teaching and
learning?

5. How do we evaluate?
Example of reports (e.g. parent
surveys, co-ordinator reports)?
Use of external validation (e.g.
LEA, NQT, NPQH, Lip, BSA)?
Ways of using performance data?
Ways of reviewing school policy?
Involvement of governors?
Celebrate achievements?

Figure 2.1 Audit of the quality of school self-review

Table 2.3 An example of a proforma for the analysis of data and target setting

EDP Reference Priority 1.1.4	*Autumn 1999 – Analysis of data and target setting*
	Primary
	Audit the quality of school self-review
	Analyse school performance data and update school profile
	Monitor performance of boys
	Agree English and maths 2002 targets for KS2 9 (year 5)
	Encourage schools to set KS1 English and maths targets (Year 1)
	Establish progress in setting individual pupil targets for literacy and numeracy
	Monitor year 4 test scores
	Establish if school is seeking to set year 4 targets for English and maths
	Monitor implementation of numeracy and literacy hours
	Identify excellence and areas of concern

The process of target setting

Section 19 of the Education Act 1997 empowered the Secretary of State to make regulations requiring school bodies to set and publish annual performance targets. 'Target Setting in Schools' (Circular 11/98) sets the context and provides practical guidance on the nature and scope of the

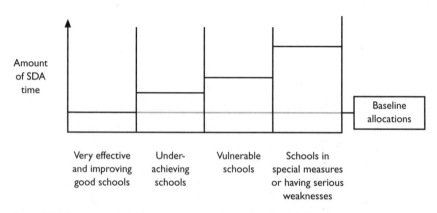

Figure 2.2 The amount of SDA time provided to schools of different standards

target-setting process. LEAs are required to hold discussions with schools about their individual targets, which are included in an annexe of the Education Development Plan, along with the LEA's own targets and programmes of support. Within this context, challenging targets in literacy and numeracy have high priority, along with progress in GCSE. This range of targets is likely to expand to include other key stages.

The Secretary of State for Education and Employment has stated:

> The second and related issue rising rapidly to the top of the emergency agenda is the education of pupils aged eleven to fourteen. I see it as essential to achieving our wider objectives at secondary level. The success at primary level in the last two years has brought into sharp focus the unacceptable lack of progress from age eleven to fourteen.
>
> (*Raising Aspirations in the 21st Century*, DfEE, January 2000)

Early national guidance on the process of school target setting included *Setting Targets to Raise Standards* (DfEE/OfSTED, 1996) and *From Targets to Action* (DfEE, 1997).

In addition, many LEAs provided further guidance based on:

- local best practice;
- the use of value-added data; and
- networking families of similar schools.

Moreover, the requirements of OfSTED school inspections also emphasised the extent to which each school's priorities for improvement were:

- the right issues to be pursuing in relation to the schools' circumstances and needs;
- clearly planned for action with appropriately targeted resources; and
- based on rigorous procedures for school self-review with the analysis of pupil performance as crucial.

In working with schools on target setting, the *Code of Practice on LEA–School Relations* (paras 61–71) indicates how LEAs and schools should work together to set and achieve challenging improvement targets.

For the LEA, the task has been:

- to gain commitment from schools to the target-setting process;
- to access effective research and information services;
- to train teachers, headteachers, governors and advisers;
- to identify and disseminate best practice;
- to discuss and agree targets with schools.

Table 2.4 LEA and Education Department target setting for schools

---

When looking to ensure sustainable growth the LEA needs to ensure that school targets are:

---

relevant and appropriate	targets reflect:	analysis of pupil population need
		character of school and its aims
		evidence of audit of progress
		internal and external evidence
rigorously well-informed	targets based on:	quality data
		shared understanding of progress
		analysis of pupil levels of attainment and progress
		knowledge of comparative attainment
imaginative, risk taking and high in expectation	targets promote:	high expectations
		teacher–pupil dialogue
		shared risk and ambition
representing underlying improvement in progress	targets show:	progress over previous year
		progress rate meets needs
achievable through identified strategies and improvement plans	targets to be achieved through:	high-quality action plans
		effective targeting of underachieving groups
		rigorous pupil assessment informing teaching

When looking to meet the LEA's agreed contribution to national targets, the Education Department needs to:

---

ensure clarity about the roles and responsibilities of LEA staff:	senior LEA staff gain commitment from all schools
	ensure coherence across the directorate
	celebrate success in achieving targets
	report progress to a range of audiences
ensure staff are well trained:	use of performance data
	– analysis
	– trends
	– use of triggers
	develop high-quality consultancy skills to challenge both successful and underachieving schools
ensure systems to monitor progress in target setting:	information flows from and to schools
	systems for analysis of data
	reports on progress
	– aggregated school target
	– key stage outcome scores
	– links to EDP priorities and success criteria
ensure a quality process	ensure quality standards for the target-setting process
	– gain feedback from:
	– headteachers
	– governors
	– staff

In all this, the key role of the Education Department has been to ensure that effective school targets:

- lead to genuine and sustainable school improvement;
- collectively meet the LEA's own agreed targets to comply with national requirements.

Those who work with schools on target setting need to ensure that the targets schools set are sufficiently challenging, relying not only on where the school has come from, but also the potential of pupils and teachers to excel or generate 'breakthrough' as O'Keefe argues in *Business Beyond the Box* (1999). O'Keefe states that too much of our thinking is constrained within the habit of incrementalism. More effective is what he describes as the process of step breakthrough. (See Figure 2.3.)

For breakthrough results, all three elements of picturing step change, developing know-how and using creative thinking must interact. The book goes on to outline strategies and tactics which have been successful in setting and achieving ambitious 'breakthrough' targets. Perhaps the LEA process of target setting needs to be informed not only by

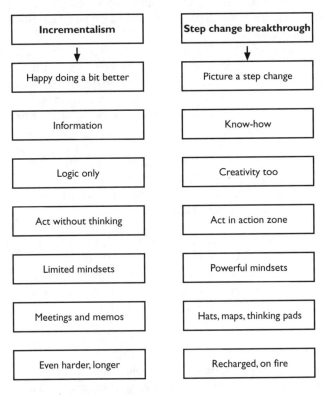

Figure 2.3 The process of step breakthrough compared to incrementalism

research into current educational practice but also the practical experiences and guidance offered by the wider professional and commercial community.

Effective systems of recording visits information

If the authority wants to know all schools it is essential that the LEA gathers information and intelligence in ways which are:

- coherent across all service areas
- reliable and consistent
- manageable.

This section will cover the ways in which the work of key school improvement staff, especially advisers and inspectors, informs how well the LEA knows its schools and ensures differentiation of resources to meet need.

In relation to school improvement, there are clear links and steps in the process of audit, setting the vision, target setting, action planning and monitoring and evaluating progress. The LEA will need to know how its resources are to be deployed, what information to gather and how to assure quality. Figure 2.4 indicates the kind of information flows that link the work of advisers.

The aim is to provide an audit trail of how the work of all advisers is clearly linked to the AIS Business Plan objectives, which themselves are a refinement of the EDP. Key elements are the matching of adviser time to activity and the monitoring arrangements to ensure targets and quality standards are met. An illustration of the allocation of differentiated adviser time is set out in Table 2.5.

Finally, as part of the monitoring of quality standards, most quality assurance models promote the importance of customer feedback. In the case of link advisers it is possible to invite feedback from headteachers, in relation to the agreed, published annual programme of visits. A proforma could cover the areas shown in Table 2.6.

In addition to performance data the outcomes of visits to schools by officers and advisers provide core information enabling the LEA to know all schools. Visit notes enable the collation of data on relevant priorities to be monitored, such as progress on literacy and numeracy action plans, and progress in the NGfL. Most visit notes also include:

- alert systems, where there are particular problems and issues for a given school; and
- good practice triggers, where examples of good school practice in teaching and learning and school organisation can be fed into an LEA register.

Table 2.5 Chart A: Allocation of target days (1999–2000)

Code			EDP activities	Advisers		
Priority	Activity	Subset	Descriptor	A.P.	R.S.	P.W.
1	1	1	Self-review			
1	1	2	Self-review – targets	20	20	16
1	1	3	Self-review – best practice	7	7	7
1	1	4	Self-review – monitoring	72	75	60
1	1	5	Self-review – teacher assessment (incl. KS1 audit, baseline, KS1/2)	4	4	
1	1	6	Self-review – underachieving schools	6	6	6
1	2	0	Literacy strategy			
1	3	0	Numeracy strategy			3
1	4	0	Raise standards of attainment in ICT			
1	5	0	Raise achievement at KS2			
1	6	0	KS2/3 continuity and progression			
1	7	0	Raise achievement of boys			
1	8	0	Raise achievement of the bottom 20%	5	5	5
2	1	0	Teacher recruitment strategy (incl. H/T appointments)	6	6	6
2	2	0	Raise the morale of teachers and governing bodies			
2	3	0	Prof. dev. links to national standards	20		15
2	4	0	Prof. dev. links to school development		14	8
2	5	0	Standards of teaching and learning			
3	1	1	New ways of working			
3	1	2	EAZ			
3	1	3	Single regeneration budget (SRB)			
3	1	4	Disadvantaged areas			
3	1	5	Combat truancy and disaffection			
3	1	6	Health promoting schools and substance misuse			
3	1	7	English as an additional language			
3	1	8	Achievement of travellers' pupils			
3	1	9	Behaviour support plan			
4	1	1	Schools vulnerable	21	7	10
4	1	2	Schools in serious weaknesses/ special measures (support)	9	15	4

Table 2.5 Continued

4	1	3	Monitoring and reporting on progress (review)	5	10	1
4	1	4	School closure			
4	1	5	Effective LEA policy			
			Schools consultancy (Buy back)			
1			Raise levels of pupil achievement generally			
			Consultancy	5	5	5
			Gov. Dev. Delivery			
3			Raise achievement in disadvantaged areas			
			Consultancy	1	1	1
4			Gov. Dev. Delivery			
			Raise performance in low-achieving schools			
			Consultancy			
			Gov. Dev. Delivery			
2			Recruit retain develop H/Ts, tchrs, govs, learning assts			
			Consultancy	8	7	
			Gov. Dev. Delivery			
			Other Activities			
5	0	0	OfSTED	4		5
6	0	0	LEA School Consortia for initial teacher training (SCITT)			
7	0	0	Billericay SCITT			
8	0	0	Other SCITT			
9	0	0	Publications editor			
10	0	0	National Professional Qualification for Headship (NPQH)			
11	0	0	IIP (TEC)			
12	1	0	INSET main programme (by priority)			37
13	0	0	Projects			
			Totals	184	182	183
			Target	180	180	180
			Difference	−4	−2	−3

Source: Essex LEA

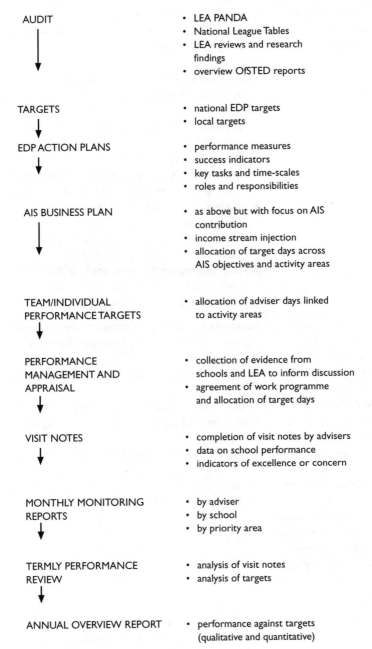

AUDIT
- LEA PANDA
- National League Tables
- LEA reviews and research findings
- overview OfSTED reports

TARGETS
- national EDP targets
- local targets

EDP ACTION PLANS
- performance measures
- success indicators
- key tasks and time-scales
- roles and responsibilities

AIS BUSINESS PLAN
- as above but with focus on AIS contribution
- income stream injection
- allocation of target days across AIS objectives and activity areas

TEAM/INDIVIDUAL PERFORMANCE TARGETS
- allocation of adviser days linked to activity areas

PERFORMANCE MANAGEMENT AND APPRAISAL
- collection of evidence from schools and LEA to inform discussion
- agreement of work programme and allocation of target days

VISIT NOTES
- completion of visit notes by advisers
- data on school performance
- indicators of excellence or concern

MONTHLY MONITORING REPORTS
- by adviser
- by school
- by priority area

TERMLY PERFORMANCE REVIEW
- analysis of visit notes
- analysis of targets

ANNUAL OVERVIEW REPORT
- performance against targets (qualitative and quantitative)

Figure 2.4 The type of information flows that link the work of advisers

Table 2.6 Chart B: Adviser quality assurance – workplan

Aspect of workplan	Qualities, skills, attributes
General	General is focused to raising standards and school improvement Can: • Engage in professional debate with you, governors and colleagues • Advise on national initiatives • Evaluate situations, and through consultancy skills work with school personnel to plan next steps • Suggest appropriate colleagues for support, advice, consultancy • Identify with you and for your strengths and weaknesses in school performance Adviser communication (visit notes/review notes/telephone, etc.) is clear, followed up and reflects the discussions undertaken
Autumn Term Analysis of data and target setting • Interrogation and interpretation of data (PANDA, OfSTED, SATs, GCSE, school data) • Benchmarking against other schools • Develop school profile based on EQF • Analysing information from performance data and agreeing targets • Monitoring progress towards previous targets	Standards and Quality Indicators to measure Senior Adviser School Development (SASD) effectiveness Adviser is: Confident and competent in the interrogation of data (1–4) Aware of your school's data profile (1–4) Challenging and supportive in target setting process (1–4) Adviser knows your school sufficiently well to inform school profiling activities Focuses discussions to improvements made, achieved and promotes further development
Spring Term School based strategic planning Review the appropriateness of the school improvement plan	Adviser is competent and confident in school improvement planning processes Adviser can evaluate, question and support planning processes Adviser references the EQF in school improvement / development planning support

Table 2.6 Continued

Check success criteria in relation to key issues for improvement	
Evaluate the quality of the plan and the likely impact on attainment with reference to the relevant sections of the review document	
Summer Term	Adviser is competent and confident in school self-review processes
Monitoring and evaluation	
Evaluate with schools their self-review processes	Monitoring of school progress is informed by quality knowledge of the school which may include observation of teaching, analysis of data, dialogue with staff
Monitor progress on post-OfSTED action plan	
Update school profile	
Identify examples of best practice	

Usually, the visit notes are linked to pre-planned proforma or frameworks which the team apply across the range of schools they are working with. Such databases are only as useful as the data held within them and, consequently, the monitoring of quality is an essential step. This includes ensuring that:

- notes are completed and entered into the database on time;
- notes or proforma are analysed to provide information to inform strategic planning;
- there is consistency of language and content.

Summary

This chapter has set out the rationale for the LEA–school improvement role in challenging and supporting schools. It has identified some of the key characteristics of effective LEAs, illustrated through approaches and case studies. To ensure effective service delivery, however, LEAs need to have clear policies and procedures for recruitment, retention and development of AIS staff. Key questions which emerge from this chapter include:

- Is there a coherent continuing professional development policy?
- Is there clarity about roles and responsibilities?
- Is there a service handbook with supporting papers linked to each aspect of the adviser's role?
- Is there succession planning?
- Is there induction, including for changed role?
- Is there a clear programme of staff development linked to core business?
- Is performance management linked to wide ranging data collection on individual and team performance?

Interlude

Working with and supporting school governors

Fran Stevens
Chair, Birmingham Governors' Forum

I am convinced that well-motivated and informed governing bodies have an essential role to play in improving the quality of education and in raising standards. In my experience, most excellent schools have excellent governing bodies. How then can we encourage and support governors in their work, how can we transform the perception that most educationalists seem to have about the effectiveness of governing bodies?

In my view, local education authorities, in their new enabling role, should be taking the lead in facilitating the work of governors. In recent years there have been examples of innovative partnerships between schools, governors and LEAs but this has been the exception rather than the rule.

In developing services for governors the *effective LEA* should take account of the following:

- the services must be based on a genuine partnership between governors and the LEA; LEA staff must *listen* to what governors are asking for;
- the services must be responsive and flexible; they must start from where governors are at and they must respond to changing demands and changing circumstances;
- the services must be inclusive; they must reach out to governors from different backgrounds and to governors with different life experiences; and
- the services must be joined up; they should support integrated ways of working in which governors work alongside headteachers and staff and other interests.

There are many different ways for LEAs to work with governors, the combination of services that is provided in each town or area will depend on local needs and priorities.

The right staff

An important starting point is for LEAs to identify suitable staff to work with and to train and support governors. The skills that are required to motivate and empower governors can be very different from the skills needed to work with teachers and other professionals. LEAs need to recruit their support staff from a range of backgrounds. It would be interesting to know how many LEAs have employed advisors that have developed their skills as a result of their experience of being a governor.

Proactive recruitment and induction

Increasingly, it is difficult to find new governors; the work is seen as being onerous and unrewarding. The *effective* LEA can play a key role in *marketing* the work of governors and in recruiting governors. A number of LEAs have run successful advertising and recruitment campaigns that have drawn in a new generation of governors.

LEAs also directly nominate a large proportion of governors. Some LEAs have opened up the nomination process; they have moved away from the traditional approach of nominations via political parties/trade unions and they have created links with a range of business and voluntary/community organisations.

LEAs should take the lead in recruiting under-represented groups, such as minority ethnic groups. There are many opportunities to reach out into communities where people often feel excluded from education and where they might lack the confidence to become involved in running their school. Special capacity building programmes have been developed, often as part of a wider approach to area regeneration. Such programmes must be sustained, since short-term initiatives can often increase disillusionment and compound the problems.

Imaginative and accessible governor training

Once people are attracted into becoming governors, it is essential that they feel valued from the outset. LEAs working with schools and with experienced governors need to offer *high-quality induction training* that gives new governors a 'flying start'.

Most LEAs offer some form of ongoing governor training programme; such programmes can be very traditional in their approach. Most governors do not want to 'return to the classroom'; they want training that is stimulating, interactive and above all enjoyable. The design of governor training programmes requires careful thought and planning. There is a place for formal courses and workshops and for one-off conferences and events. But other approaches should also be considered; whole-school training can be very effective with governors working alongside staff and other local interests. Specialist training is also needed for governors who take on specific roles such as chairs, treasurers, SEN governors and so on. A number of accredited training programmes are available for governors but these are not necessarily being accessed by the people who might benefit from them the most.

Training programmes should be reviewed regularly by the LEA with governors. As new needs emerge and new responsibilities are placed on governors then new programmes have to be designed. The 'same old programme' should not be rolled out year on year.

Relevant and understandable information and guidance for governors

Governing bodies are deluged with paperwork; every month brings new government guidelines and initiatives. The *effective LEA* has an important role in explaining and interpreting all of these government directives and initiatives. In addition, they must provide clear information on their own services/policies. There are some innovative ways of tackling the information explosion; there is a great emphasis on 'wiring up' schools but governors and governing bodies have not normally been included in such information networks. It would be interesting to see how all governors could be linked up to their schools and to each other.

Specialist support and conflict resolution for schools in difficulty

Governing bodies require access to specialist advisors from time to time. Assistance is needed in many areas including:

- the implementation of new policies/programmes, such as performance management;
- personnel matters such as recruiting a new headteacher; and
- financial management and control.

Every now and then governing bodies require intensive support; it could be a school under special measures, a school faced with serious behaviour problems or a school where there are serious conflicts within the governing body or between the governing body and the head and staff. In these instances the LEA needs to be able to intervene sensitively and skilfully. Advisors working in these situations need skills in mediation and conflict resolution.

Support for governor networks and forums

Increasingly governing bodies and governors need to learn from each other, they need to be able to network and to share ideas and experiences. There are also times when governors require a collective voice. LEAs have often resisted the development of such structures as they feared a challenge to their authority. The educational world is changing and there are now good reasons for LEAs to work with governors to build up local networks. Beyond this, it should be a requirement on all LEAs to facilitate the formation of a representative body of governors. Many LEAs do support a governors' forum or a similar body but there are many others that have not seen this as a priority.

Meaningful involvement in policy making and in special initiatives

LEAs can and should consult governors over the development and implementation of local education policies. Such consultation has to be meaningful; it is not enough to circulate consultation documents. Consultative events may need to be organised and if working groups are established they should meet at times/places that are convenient for governors. Governor forums are another mechanism for ensuring that governors can participate effectively in policy making. Governors should take their place on formal committees and decision-making groups; tokenism must be avoided and every effort should be made to involve and engage governors.

The governor-friendly LEA

LEAs face an uncertain future. Their 'top-down' approach has been brought into question and their powers and resources have increasingly been devolved down to schools. Many have found it difficult to adapt to an enabling role and they still face criticism for being wasteful and out of touch. There are, however, ways in which LEAs can reinvent themselves. Governors and governing bodies need continuing assistance if they are to carry out the full range of their responsibilities. A responsive and imaginative LEA should be able to develop excellent services for governors; services that governors will value and that they will wish to continue to use, as they and their schools take more control over the purchasing of services.

In future, the *effective LEA* will have to be a *governor-friendly LEA*.

3 Raising standards through the Education Development Plan

Diane Simmonds

> The combination of Education Development Plans and OfSTED inspections will provide a comprehensive system for ensuring that LEAs promote high standards in schools and will contribute to the Best Value review process for local government as a whole
>
> (DfEE Draft Guidance on EDPs, 1998)

There can be no doubt that the government places education at the top of the political agenda ... as Tony Blair emphasised at his Oxford speech in 1999: 'the endowments of our children are literally the most precious of the natural resources of the community and that the government should give proper leadership and take proper responsibility for educational standards'. He highlighted that this meant three things for the government.

- Taking national responsibility for investment in raising standards by placing education at the top of the government's list.
- Setting clear goals – the most fundamental being an education system combining diversity with excellence and ensuring high standards for everyone in the basics in primary schools.
- Being very robust about the opportunities post-16.

Many partners will make a contribution to this ambitious agenda but only schools can deliver its core aims; they have the prime responsibility for raising standards and school improvement.

However, local education authorities (LEAs) have a key role both strategically and operationally; their partnership with schools is crucial in implementing much of the government's 'standards agenda'. This responsibility was originally stated in the 1997 White Paper *Excellence in Schools*, which detailed six core tasks for LEAs, and a vision of the new style of partnership between LEAs and schools. The Standards and Framework Act 1998, Section 5 later defined the LEAs' statutory duty as 'to carry out their functions to promote high standards'. The challenge now is for LEAs and schools to develop a partnership which has as its core function a high-quality education for all pupils, whilst retaining value for money and accountability.

Education Development Plans (EDPs) are the LEA's strategic plan for delivering school improvement and raising standards; they are the prime manifestation of their statutory duty. For the first time in ten years LEAs are required to place raising the standards of pupils attainment at the centre of their services. Although nationally and locally this change in an LEA's core task may take time to embed, it will extend and enhance the school improvement policies, actions, strategies and research which characterised the previous work in LEAs and higher education institutions, such as Birmingham, Suffolk, Kirklees, Keele and ULIE.

This new partnership for raising standards is summed up in the introduction to the Milton Keynes Education Development Plan summary leaflet for schools, parents and the wider community which states: 'It is the schools' headteachers, teachers, supports staff and governors, supported by parents and the community, who will make the difference and improve standards. Staff from the LEA and its partners will provide focused support (and challenge).'

ZPD

Education development plans – what is their strategic role and purpose?

> Education Development Plans are designed to focus the efforts of Local Education Authorities and schools as they work together to improve standards. LEAs and schools must identify what needs to be done to drive up performance and who will do it. A key element of this process will be the setting of targets for pupil achievement in each school. The EDP is the strategic plan for LEA action to improve standards, but does not cover activity funded and managed at school level, although that will be a relevant background. A shared agenda and agreed objectives between LEAs and their schools is crucial to the success of the EDP.
>
> (DfEE Education Development Plan Guidance, Sept. 1998)

The law defines the twin purposes of the EDP as:

- to raise standards of education for all children in LEA maintained schools.
- to improve the performance of schools maintained by the LEAs.

The main roles of the EDP are:

- to provide the LEA with a strategic plan for schools improvement;
- to be the plan against which LEA's support for school improvement will be inspected by OfSTED;

- to provide the focus for work that the LEA, with schools, will undertake to raise standards and contribute to school improvement.

The plan is in two parts:

Part one requires the approval of the Secretary of State and includes:

- the statutory **LEA targets** up to 2002 for pupil performance at Key
Stage 2 and Key Stage 4; improving the attainment of looked-after
children; and reducing absence and exclusion;
- the LEA school improvement programme of between 5–8 priorities.
The aim is to assist the LEA to achieve targets, address weaknesses
and enhance identified strengths, as well as deliver national priorities
such as the National Literacy Strategy, National Numeracy Strategy
and the Social Inclusion agenda. This programme must show how it is
derived from a local audit of strengths and weaknesses;
- the LEA's strategy for schools causing concern and how the activities
in the plan will support this.

Part two is seven annexes which make up the supporting information
including:

- tables showing performance targets for each maintained school;
- the LEA's context, and an audit of strengths, weaknesses and needs;
- an action plan for each activity in the school improvement programme, including success criteria, target groups and monitoring
procedures;
- a summary of the LEA's plan to improve standards for pupils with SEN;
- the resources to be allocated to the school improvement programme;
- a strategy for monitoring and evaluating the plan;
- the report on the LEA's consultation on the plan.

The core aim of the plan is to ensure that all pupils receive a good education whilst recognising that schools have the prime responsibility for
improvement. The LEA's plan sets out their strategy for monitoring, challenging and supporting schools in raising standards. EDPs are different
from previous plans in that they have a strong government steer about the
required level of targets set for each LEA, a clear focus on teaching and
learning and the expectation that the plan will include national initiatives
to raise standards. They are about action and activity more than structure
and processes.

Many of the strategies for school improvement are nationally prescribed
and this was a source of tension for LEAs as they developed the first
plan. Many plans look similar as the NFER/EMIE report 'Education
Development Plans Meeting Targets and Improving Schools Role' (1999)

notes: 'LEAs were bound fairly tightly in the priorities they were able to choose, and it is not surprising that those presented were common to most EDPs'. However, within the local context there is still room for the LEA and schools to decide the why, the what, the how, the when, by whom and so what?

Most LEAs and senior officers agree that the process of developing this strategic school improvement plan has been crucial and influential in reinforcing the school improvement agenda and has frequently acted as the lever for implementing change. The level of planning based on identified need ensures that raising standards is core to the overall strategy of a council.

It is also important for the plan to fit into the other strategic plans of the authority. Where an LEA maps the links between their EDP, the authority's other plans, best-value principles and LEA inspection, the power to make a real difference to standards and school improvement is evident.

What makes a strategically effective plan?

A plan that:
- never loses sight of its purpose to raise pupils' achievements;
- enables the continuous improvement of schools;
- uses clear evidence to structure the plan, including an audit, LEA profiles and benchmarking;
- targets not only the performance of the LEA, its schools and individual pupils, but ensures support for specific underachieving groups of pupils, schools, teachers or subjects;
- has action plans which are clearly focused on teaching and learning, and classroom practice;
- shares good and interesting practice and articulates what works well;
- celebrates improvement;
- tackles failure clearly and effectively;
- purposefully ensures sustained improvement;
- ensures effective monitoring;
- has systematic and robust evaluation particularly involving schools and other agencies;
- promotes high-quality school self-evaluation and review with effective links between school development/improvement plans and the Education Development Plan.

The key development of an effective Education Development Plan which fulfils its strategic purpose of raising standards can be summed up by the now familiar 'Cycle of LEA support for school improvement' (Figure 3.1).

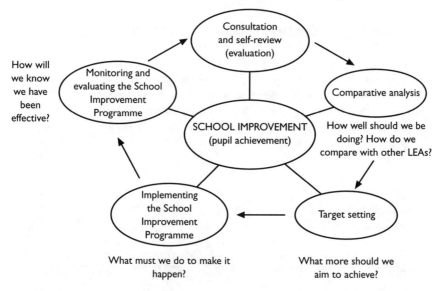

Figure 3.1 Cycle of LEA support, challenge and monitoring for school improvement

How well should we be doing? How do we compare with other LEAs?

The DfEE guidance requires the Education Development Plan to have a brief statement about the key characteristics of the LEA, which sets the local context and is relevant to raising standards and school improvement. It also requires an overview and audit of pupil, school and LEA performance. Although a 'succinct summary of the key factors' was asked for; most LEAs provide a detailed and frequently excellent self analysis. The context and audit statement have proved to be essential when defining the rationale for setting targets; deciding the priorities, actions and activities of the school improvement programme, and developing the strategy for schools causing concern. An annual review of this audit is crucial in determining progress and refocusing LEA actions to raise standards.

A good EDP School Improvement Programme is one where the priorities and associated activities are derived from: a thorough and honest audit of performance, a clear identification of strengths and weaknesses and one that reflects the LEA's contextual framework.

LEA context statements are a reminder of the difficulties faced by some authorities as well as a reminder that there are pockets of deprivation in predominately affluent authorities. As extracts on page 43 illustrate.

Greenwich Education Development Plan 1999–2002
Fringe of south-east and inner London. Ranked the 11th most deprived LEA in England, but has pockets of high affluence in Blackheath and Greenwich. One in four persons live in poverty. Eighteen per cent of pupils speak English as an additional language; 104 children come from traveller families. There are unacceptable levels of racism, 56 per cent of the population commutes to work. High levels of lone parent families and percentage of pupils living in overcrowded conditions. The council spends over SSA.

Cambridgeshire Education Development Plan, 1999–2002
Predominantly rural, but the fastest growth rate in the country. There is a significant traveller population. The county is prosperous but with pockets of deprivation. Twelve per cent of primary schools have less than 100 pupils. There are variable post-16 staying on rates. Low Standard Spending Assessment (SSA).

The context of an LEA is the framework not an excuse for the Plan, often providing a rationale for choices made in its overall strategy.

The audit or annual review of performance and standards makes significant use of comparative data at all levels; LEA, schools and pupils. It identifies the strengths and weaknesses of pupils, school and the LEA. This is vital in ensuring that the EDP provides an effective school improvement programme which targets resources on the specific groups of schools, pupils, teachers and subjects that will contribute to:

- raising standards of attainment;
- improving the quality of the education provided by schools.

The audit of pupil, school and LEA performance is the evidential base for deciding the priorities, activities and actions which contribute to LEAs school improvement programme. The activity action plans will cover significant weaknesses and aim to secure improvement in: pupils standards, teaching and learning, leadership, management and governance whilst also reflecting the implications of the LEA statutory targets.

The main sources of evidence for a good audit includes information and analysis from:

- the OfSTED LEA profile, which provides data on the performance of LEAs, schools and pupils. Comparisons are given of performance compared to the national picture and benchmarking against

statistical neighbours, including performance and inspection information;
- the Advisory and Inspection Service monitoring of schools – programmes of monitoring visits including annual reviews;
- the LEA-produced data and information, analysis of raw and value-added data;
- evidence from school self-evaluation, including improvement priorities from the school's development plans;
- the analysis of OfSTED inspection of school report;
- the QCA statistical material;
- the DfEE Autumn package – detailed new and value added information setting school performance into a variety of contexts;
- OfSTED school profiles (PANDAs) – which look in more depth at a school's specific strengths and weaknesses. Provides national and benchmark contexts for detailed performance information and previous inspection judgement.

The use of statistical neighbour comparisons in the LEA's OfSTED profile and the benchmarking contexts for OfSTED school profiles require some understanding of a still developing system of reliable statistical neighbours. Whilst not an excuse for lower standards they do present a challenge to LEAs and schools that are performing less well than similar LEAs and schools.

The extracts below shows just some of the evidence which will inform where the particular LEA focuses its work for school improvement.

Kingston upon Thames LEA: extract from its 1990–2000 audit and annual review of standards:
- practice in Kingston schools is good overall and in many respects we are better than our statistical neighbours (LEA OfSTED profile)
- the quality of teaching overall is good and better than the OfSTED findings for schools nationally and in our statistical neighbours
- standards at KS2 in more than half of our primary schools are below the QCA median benchmark (Autumn Package)
- there is a wide variation in performance between schools, with significant difference in subject outcomes in the same school.
- there are significant differences in the achievement of boys and girls. With boys underachieving from a young age and attaining less well than girls as they get older, particularly in English.

Greenwich LEA: extract from their 1999–2000 annual report of performance
Performance of specific groups of pupils

- The performance of boys lagged behind that of girls in reading, writing and English at all Key Stages and GCSE. In maths and science the performance of boys and girls was very similar.
- Pupils eligible for free school meals performed less well than the borough average at all ages and in all subjects.
- Bangladeshi pupils were well below the borough average at the ends of Key Stage 1 and 2 but were above the borough average at Key Stage 3 and GCSE.
- Turkish/Turkish Cypriot pupils were well below the borough average at the ends of Key Stage 1, 2 and 3 but above for GCSE.
- Vietnamese pupils were below the borough average for reading and writing at Key Stage 1, but above for all other ages.
- Chinese and Indian pupils performed better than the borough average at every age in all subjects.
- The gaps between the performance of girls and boys were most marked in the following ethnic groups: Bangladeshi, Black African, Black Caribbean, Black Other, Chinese, Indian, Mixed Origin, Pakistani, Vietnamese.

It is crucial for the LEA to focus its school improvement programme activities on supporting the weaknesses to be addressed and achieving the outcome targets set.

What more should we aim to achieve? Setting targets

Governing bodies are legally responsible for setting and publishing targets for the performance of their pupils at ages 11 and 16 in relation to National Curriculum assessment and public examinations.

The government and LEAs have also set targets for 2002, and schools are expected to support the achievement of these. National targets set by the Secretary of State for 2002 Key Stage 2 English and mathematics and Key Stage 4 were followed by the setting of 'top–down' targets for LEAs in consultation with the DfEE. The targets for both the LEA and the schools are a significant section of the EDP and define an important quantitative outcome of a successful plan.

The EDP requires a clear statement from the LEA about how they will support and what challenge they will apply to schools in setting and meeting their targets for raising standards. Schools and in some cases LEAs have found it difficult to move away from the 'comfort zone targets' and set more aspirational targets. Schools are reasonably expert at predicting pupils' future performance in relation to attainment but they often find it hard to add the challenge or potential improvement element.

The NFER study 'The LEA Contribution to School Improvement' (July 2000) discovered that whilst target setting is crucial to sustained school improvement and identifying the groups of children who need targeted action, it is one which elicits much anxiety. These concerns focus around the publication, scrutiny and interpretation of results. It is about fear of failing; it is about payment by results; it is about interpreting a target as something you have to meet. Comments include: 'Why should we set ourselves up to fail?' (Chair of Governors); 'You have to be brave to set targets you may not hit' (Special School Headteacher); 'The worry is if you set your sights too high you will be criticised for not quite getting there' (Deputy Headteacher).

LEAs are working hard with schools and governing bodies on developing the target-setting process; providing training in the use and interpretation of data, and embedding the process in the day to day teaching, planning and assessment.

However, an EDP's school improvement programme is more effective in those LEAs and schools where challenging aspirational targets have been set, alongside a clear identification of the strengths and weaknesses in performance. The LEA is able to target its action plans more accurately and effectively to specific pupils, groups, schools, key stages and aspects of the curriculum which require support to improve and aspire to a better standard.

What must we do to make it happen? Implementing the school improvement programme

Having carried out a thorough audit to identify strengths, weaknesses and aspects for improvement, an effective EDP will focus the priorities, activities and action plans of its school improvement programme on:

* those aspects of the LEA's school improvement work which will raise standards;
* targeting groups of pupils, schools, teachers and subjects which have an impact on raising standards;
* setting success criteria which aim to raise standards.

In early 1999 prior to statutory approval by the Secretary of State, the DfEE Standards and Effectiveness Unit assessed the quality of all EDPs and the more frequently quoted weaknesses were as follows: 'more of the activities need to be targeted specifically to identified schools; key stages or groups of pupils'; 'the statement on schools causing concern needs to be linked more directly to the action plans; the scale and extent of action needs to be clarified'; 'the audit is thorough and sets out identified weaknesses; annex 3 (action plans) however is rather diffuse – and many activities lack specific focus'. This initial feedback and the subsequent rolling forward of the EDP into 2000–1 has resulted in more focused action plans which target those schools, groups of pupils or phases that will benefit from the LEA's support and challenge.

If raising standards is about improving teaching and learning then the most successful School Improvement Programmes ensure that the LEA's actions focus on underachieving groups of pupils, schools, teachers, subjects and aspects of the curriculum. Pedagogy, pupils, curriculum and leadership are at the heart of raising standards for these underachieving groups as well as ensuring 'continuing improvement' overall.

The following case study represents good practice in focused action plans and targeting specific groups. It brings together the identification of underachieving groups and schools through the audit, the school improvement plan, the annual review of performance and the target-setting process.

Kingston upon Thames LEA – case study. The LEA traditionally scored well above the national average league tables based on pupil performance. There had not, however, been a culture of school challenge to explore what further gains in standards could be achieved. Their school improvement strategy, of which the Education Development Plan is its core document, is designed to raise standards for all pupils and to ensure greater rigour and challenge in the context of target setting and self-valuating schools.

Priority C of Kingston's Education Development Plan is to 'raise the achievement of boys and girls and improve the progress of lower attaining pupils'.

The focus of this priority has been to support schools to address gender issues, especially the underachievement of boys; to improve behaviour and attendance; to support bilingual learning; to develop work-related opportunities in the curriculum and to seek additional resources for supporting socially deprived pupils. One of the activities was specifically to 'support target setting to reduce the gender gap in the achievement of boys and girls at each key stage'. The Numeracy and Literacy Strategies are already raising awareness of the gender gap through its training and support programme to schools.

What was planned? (Focus of activity)
In the current cycle of target setting, significant attention was given to what value schools were adding in relation to prior attainment. Using a Kingston measure of value added and the analysis of CATs scores, it became clear that a significant minority of primary schools were achieving below expectation. This finding was reinforced by looking at the Qualifications and Curriculum Authority (QCA) data, which enabled benchmarking similar groups of schools against free school meals.

What was done? (Actions)

The initial task was to ensure that all primary schools were clear about the performance of Kingston Schools not only through national perspectives, but more importantly through comparison with other like schools. Headteacher and governor meetings and link inspector visits were used to develop a culture which helped schools to self-assess against best performance and to be aware of whether they were performing above, at, or below expectation.

For the autumn term programme of target setting the LEA provided individual pupil data for all schools. This was to be analysed in addition to the Autumn Pack. In working with schools, the approach of link inspectors was as follows:

- to be aware of some of the difficulties and sensitivities emerging from the OfSTED gradings of schools, based on free school meals (FSM) groupings;
- to allow schools to set and justify their own targets based on a challenging dialogue about the potential of each individual pupil;
- to ensure that schools could demonstrate how target setting had informed teacher planning through curriculum targets and assessment outcomes for each pupil.

What has been the impact? (Success criteria)

- Most primary schools have greater confidence in target setting and are using performance data to set more challenging targets. In the current cycle, the aggregated schools targets matches that of the LEA.
- Teacher skills in assessing pupil performance, setting learning targets and matching these to curriculum plans and targets has improved. In classrooms, teachers have adopted a 'critical steps' approach through the National Curriculum levels and have become more rigorous in matching the learning to identified need.
- Detailed analysis of all primary school performance, but especially that of the underachieving schools has shown that boys' under-performance is an issue. The issue of school underachievement was linked closely to boys' underachievement.

Next steps – rolling the action plans forward

The LEA has published its strategy for addressing gender differences in learning and attainment which it hopes will support underachieving schools to raise standards. There are three elements:

- a focus on pupil assessment and pupil performance tracking, with pupil targets for individuals and groups of boys;
- a better teacher understanding of learning styles, closely linked to developments in literacy and numeracy;
- a consideration of school ethos – creating a culture which encourages boys to do better, linked to a greater understanding of behaviour and attitude.

Similar good quality work of raising standards through well-targeted support and challenge is found in the EDP of many LEAs, e.g. Newham, Tower Hamlets, Shropshire and North Yorkshire.

The overall impact of a good school improvement programme will be demonstrated through improved pupil performance, less exclusions, improved attendance, a shorter time to turn around failing schools, and an improved quality of education.

How will we know we have been effective? Monitoring and evaluating the School Improvement Programme

A statement of how the LEA intends to monitor and evaluate its EDP is one of the required annexes of supporting information. In the first year this has been a dominant feature of an LEA's work at both the micro-level of individual activity action plans and the macro-level of maintaining a strategic overview of targets, the school improvement programme and the schools causing concern strategy.

The purpose of the EDP monitoring and evaluation statement is to show 'how the LEA will monitor achievement against each target, priority and activity including the use of resources' (*EDP Guidance*, DfEE, September 1999).

In the first year a substantial part of the monitoring and evaluation of the EDP has been undertaken internally. There have been four distinct aspects of this process:

1   monitoring the progress of the activity action plans;
2   monitoring pupil and school performance, including specific groups and the quality of teaching and learning;
3   consulting stakeholders on the effectiveness of the plan;
4   evaluating the plan's effectiveness and success, including reviewing priorities.

Monitoring progress of activity action plans of the School Improvement Programme

Most LEAs have developed appropriate strategies and procedures for monitoring activities and reporting to members and stakeholders.

The strategies make good use of both paper and information technology to record progress and track activities. They are clear about who is responsible for the monitoring. Good practice ensures that the process and strategies are integral to individual officers and team work plans, as well as allowing senior managers and members to gain a strategic overview. The systems used are most effective when they are part of the overall monitoring and evaluation system of the LEA and now incorporate a Best Value Review. Methods of monitoring progress vary as the illustrations show.

Merton LEA used the original action plan format and the lead officer records progress alongside each heading in both electronic and written form.

Action Plan Heading	Monitoring Progress
• Purpose	
• Nature of activity	
• Target groups	• Implications re: further activity
• Action to be taken	• Tasks completed to date
• Start date, completion and responsibility	• Tasks to be rescheduled
• Success criteria	• Success evidence
• Monitoring evaluation	• Monitoring undertaken
• Resource	• Budget spent to date

Cambridgeshire LEA used a termly monitoring sheet to be completed by each activity leader which maps and records responses to the following points:

• operational monitoring – is the activity action plan complete; are there any impediments?
– revisions to the implementation
• quality monitoring – was the activity satisfactory completed? is there any evidence of satisfaction or dissatisfaction from schools, if so what?
• progress or realisation of the EDP targets
• progress on finance; what is the spending to date?
• next steps; is there different action required to achieve the priority and activity?
• what are the emerging issues?

Buckinghamshire LEA used an 'at a glance' system of red, amber, green for tracking progress and giving an overall view of 'how we are doing':
• green is for tasks progressing according to schedule;
• amber is for tasks where there may be some progress;
• red where there are major problems and intervention is needed.

These monitoring procedures are common to many authorities thereby allowing regular reports to be made to members and to schools, as well as ensuring linkage between the wide variety of LEA Plans and teams. In the long term the monitoring systems will allow effective quality assurance of service delivery.

The most effective monitoring systems allow LEAs to:

• be alert to identify over or under use of resources both financial and personnel;

- review the focus of school improvement over the coming year;
- celebrate success and identify good practice in raising standards;
- gather evidence for funding the efficiency of delivery;
- re-schedule activities;
- identify when performance targets are not being met.

Monitoring of pupil and school performance

The vast majority of LEAs undertake an annual review of pupil attainment at Key Stages 1, 2, 3, 4 and Post-16. The analysis of pupil attainment identifies strengths and weaknesses in performance, thereby ensuring LEAs focus their EDP activities more precisely on actions which will raise pupils standards, improve the teaching and learning and contribute to effective school improvement.

In those LEAs which have developed good practice the annual review of pupil performance includes:

- analysis by gender, ethnicity, SEN and mobility.
- identification of where pupils are underperforming or have weaknesses, e.g. writing at Key Stage 2, modern foreign languages or design and technology at Key Stage 4.
- identifying the professional development needs of both teachers and LEA advisers/officers for improving the use and interpretation of assessment data.

This monitoring of pupil and school performance is frequently the basis of annual reports by chief inspectors to wider audiences and is part of the LEA's overall strategy for ensuring accountability. A strength of many authorities is the quality of this annual report, to members, schools and governing bodies which is now being set alongside an overview of the OfSTED school inspections for the year and the monitoring of progress for their EDP.

What do our stakeholders say about our effectiveness?

In addition to robust internal monitoring and evaluation systems covering both activity action plans and pupil and school performance, there is increasing use of other methods of monitoring and evaluation involving stakeholders.

At the end of the first year an increasing number of LEAs are using school questionnaires to:

- review their Education Development Plans and activities;
- monitor implementation and involvement in activities;
- evaluate the impact of the school improvement programme on pupil standards and school improvement.

For example:

Greenwich LEA in March 2000 asked all their schools:
1   are our priorities still right?
2   should any be deleted?
3   should any be added?
4   which of the eight LEA priorities are in your own School Development Plan?

Milton Keynes LEA have gone one step further and asked for feedback on each activity and a comment on which of the activities are important to the school.

For each activity schools were asked to assess the involvement and impact using a four-point scale:

Involvement:
1   Strong school involvement
2   Involvement
3   Not involved
4   Not applicable

Impact:
1   Strong impact on the school
2   Some impact
3   No impact
4   Not applicable

In these examples the evaluation will be both subjective and based on perception. However, if LEAs are to ensure that their support for school improvement is effective, valued, appropriate and understood, this two-way communication with schools is vital. Lack of involvement by schools with the LEAs agenda for school improvement might signal everything from the need for intervention, inappropriate action by the LEA, or an attitude that the school needs no support as it is already successful – a pity as dissemination of best practice is a crucial feature of school improvement.

Increasingly, LEAs are using the LEA OfSTED inspection questionnaire as a baseline assessment of their effectiveness in supporting and challenging school improvement. The key questions which underpin good LEA monitoring processes are as follows:

- are we doing what we said we would do?
- is the monitoring integral to the work of the Inspection and Advisory Service and other LEA services?
- what strategies is the LEA using to monitor the progress, delivery and implementation of the school improvement programme?
- how well are we monitoring school performance (including teaching and learning), the performance of pupils (in particular specific groups), the performance of the LEA services.

- how well does the monitoring feed into the review of the plan?
- how effectively do we monitor stakeholder's involvement and attitudes?

The importance of the monitoring and evaluation is best illustrated when it is part of the day to day work of the LEA and not a bolt on activity once a year or at regular intervals. This is now more fully recognised by LEAs; for example Oxfordshire has developed an internal handbook for Monitoring and Evaluating their EDP which usefully sets out the guidance principles (self-evaluation, partnerships, best values and business excellence model); procedures; the process of data collection and analysis; timescales; reporting arrangements and key personnel responsibilities. (See Figure 3.2.)

Oxfordshire's handbook complements the arrangements for monitoring and evaluation set out in Annexe 6 of their EDP and as they state: 'The two key components of their process' are:

- monitoring the outcomes from schools as evidence of progress towards targets.
- evaluating the impact and effectiveness of various services of the Education Department in achieving the success criteria.

How effective is the plan?

The evaluations of the effectiveness and impact of the Education Development Plan are beginning to develop but will crucially depend on whether standards have risen over time and schools have improved. Good practice in evaluating the effectiveness of the school improvement programme will include evaluating the extent to which:

- the targets set by schools are being achieved;
- the success criteria for each priority in the plan are being achieved;
- the LEA's actions are having an impact in meeting the success criteria for each activity in the Plan;
- schools identified as causing concern have improved;
- the LEA's systems for identifying schools causing concern are leading to early intervention, support, challenge and consequent improvement;
- the annual audit of LEA school and pupil performance shows overall improvement compared with national rates and 'statistical neighbours';
- schools see the Plan as having overall coherence and co-ordination in providing improvement.

By monitoring the progress of the EDP and by evaluating the impact and effectiveness, LEAs are employing an important means of translating the

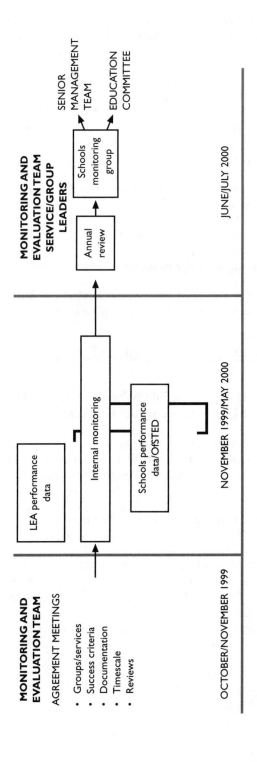

Figure 3.2 Oxfordshire: monitoring EDP progress

strategic plan for school improvement into the every day working practices throughout the authority. This is achieved best when the process and procedures are:

- integral to the LEA's self-evaluation and reviews;
- a regular part of members' agenda;
- contributing to the authority's best value review process;
- part of the on going dialogue in the LEA/school partnership;
- securely linking pupil and school's performance to the actions for school improvement.

Monitoring and evaluating the Education Development Plan must always return to the key questions:

- Are pupils receiving a good education?
- Are standards improving?
- Are schools sustaining improvement?

This continuous review of the EDP purpose is essential if they are to fulfil their potential for being the LEA's strategic plan for raising standards.

What of the future? Partnerships with schools and other agencies

Partnership in the delivery of the Education Development Plan is a requirement for developing EDPs and is essential for their future development.

> EDPs will draw together the main action which the LEA is taking in pursuit of this duty ('carry out all their functions to promote high standards') and will increase accountability to schools, to local partners and to the Government.
>
> LEAs must earn their place in the new Partnership.
>
> (*Excellence in Schools*, DFEE, 1997).

An important part of this partnership has been the consultation requirements of the EDP and the development of a new partnership between the LEA and schools, schools and schools, LEA officers and members, schools and governing bodies.

The Audit Commission report *Held in Trust: the LEA of the Future* (1999) identified four models of an LEA:

- minimalist – *laissez-faire* LEA
- traditionalist – controlling LEA
- enabling – reactive LEA
- partnership – proactive LEA.

Those LEAs that have developed or are moving towards the 'partnership' model will find it easier to raise standards through their EDP. Schools in general understand and welcome how they are supported, challenged and monitored. There is still some reluctance from some schools to be challenged to improve either because of their context or they feel they are already doing well. However, this fails to understand that in future, partnerships to promote high standards require all involved to have roles and responsibilities. Partnership with schools is also essential in the effective delivery of national policy initiatives such as Beacon Schools, Education Action Zones and Excellence in Cities programmes.

Partnership is not only with schools but frequently with either agencies, e.g. Teacher Training Agency, OfSTED, DfEE, Higher Education Institutes and private contractors to either work together on an initiative such as National Literacy Strategy, National Numeracy Strategy, or provide a brokered service to schools.

All the national initiatives, which aim to raise standards of pupil achievement and improve schools, need to be built into an LEA's EDP. This enables the strategic planning to be sustained and prevents specific initiatives detracting attention away from the core purpose. One of the powerful tools for making this a reality is to ensure that the EDP, school development planning process and target setting are linked.

How does the LEA plan for school improvement link with the School Improvement Plan?

The failure of some schools to recognise the significance and relevance of the EDP is a main issue raised by the NFER study *The LEA Contribution to School Improvement* (2000).

The speed of development in 1998–9 of the EDP alongside Fair Funding, target setting and the new Code of Practice on LEA – a School Relationships has meant that, although consultation with schools and other stakeholders over the content of the EDP was significant, establishing a strong link between the EDP and school development plan is just beginning to develop.

In 1998 when developing their EDPs LEAs sought information from schools about their school improvement priorities.

Cambridgeshire LEA for example requested all schools to identify three key priorities for school improvement, which then informed their audit and subsequent school improvement programme. It also allowed schools within the authority to link their own priorities and funding of professional development more effectively to that of the LEA.

Some individual schools have made the link, for example a primary school in Milton Keynes shows in their School Improvement Plan how the 1999 EDP priorities link to each of their school improvement priorities.

This was particularly useful because to quote the headteacher: 'it has made us focus more on school improvement matter, both curriculum and quality of teaching and learning' and 'the access to LEA support (and challenge) is now more transparent. We can see how good the LEA service is in supporting our work'.

Many LEAs are now realising the need to make the EDP a 'living document' for their schools as the illustrations show.

Merton LEA's school effectiveness team, in 2000 analysed School Development Plan themes against the EDP. They were then able to identify where the links were strong and weak.

Strong Links	**Weak links**
• raising standards in literacy and numeracy • development of ICT • raising quality of teaching • improving monitoring and role of co-ordinators • best match between EDP and SDP was in the middle phase	• high attainers • attendance • behaviour/exclusion • MFL, RE, work-related curriculum • weakest match between EDP priorities and high school SDPs

Their aim is to ensure that schools who are responsible for improvement are better placed to reflect in their own development/improvement plans the outcome of analyses by both schools and the LEA.

Worcestershire LEA has a strategy for making the EDP 'A Living Document in the LEA Schools' with the aim of ensuring real involvement of their schools. Many of their strategies are replicated across the country but are worth highlighting as an example of raising awareness and developing a partnership. They include:

• summary EDP posters for the staff room to raise teachers, governors and parent governor awareness;
• summary leaflet for a range of stakeholders;
• cross-referencing all in-service and associated activities to the EDP priority activity within which it is based. Also a poster showing each training opportunity under eight priority headings. This is well received and to quote: 'informal feedback from schools indicated that the activity reference, associated poster and detailed description of intended outcomes have led to more efficient targeting of resources and in developing School Development Plans linked to the EDP';
• contact visit schedule including structured discussion about the evaluation of the EDP and links to their SDP;
• analysis of school development plans;

- using associate headteachers more closely in the monitoring and evaluation;
- conferences and high profile events.

These strategies are ensuring that the EDP is not just another LEA Service Plan but is the strategic plan which places raising standards at the core of the work of the LEA education agenda. The linking of EDP and school development plans is an essential part of the LEA's role of monitoring and challenging standards of education within their schools.

The new standards agenda has refocused the role of LEA inspectors and advisers and whilst the LEAs have developed their own specific methods of working all have the following core tasks when monitoring schools (including school visits) to ensure they promote high standards:

- review and monitoring of performance; analysis and interpretation of data;
- support and challenge for target setting;
- monitoring of initiatives such as the National Numeracy Strategy, National Literacy Strategy, Key Stage Three Pilot Project and the strands of Excellence in Cities;
- reinforcing the link between the school development/improvement plan and the EDP;
- monitoring the quality of teaching where appropriate;
- validating school self-evaluation.

The significance of the EDP is also recognised by OfSTED in its 'Framework for Inspection of LEA Support for School Improvement' and the subsequent published report. The aim of inspection as stated in the Framework is to review and report on the way LEAs perform their functions and in particular to determine the contributions LEA's support including support to individual pupils (makes) to school improvements and to high standards of achievement. The EDP and its implementation is the key document and evidence for judging how effective is the support for school improvement. The Audit Commission's questionnaire to schools also asks 11 questions related to the EDP, its relevance and impact.

The recent OfSTED Draft Paper *Local Education Authority Support for School Improvement* (June 2000) whilst stating that the 45 inspections were all prior to EDPs being implemented it noted that 'in every case the EDP was better than what had been in place previously. The requirement to submit a plan had forced LEAs to undertake a detailed audit of needs, set clear priorities and quantifiable targets and establish a more precisely defined role in relation to school improvement'. As the Oxfordshire LEA report states:

The EDP sets out a suitable strategy for school improvement.

One of the main strengths of the plan lies in the detail of its implementation and evaluation.

The translation of the plan into action is through the generally high quality individual Service Plans that are cross referenced to the EDP priorities and are to be evaluated against the achievement of those priorities.

OfSTED recognises that the EDP is 'the LEA's principal mechanism for raising its standards'.

Overall the future is about working in partnership with schools and other stakeholders to ensure that the EDP fulfils its strategic purpose of raising standards and school improvement. The EDP is a potentially powerful LEA school improvement plan, in that it continuously refocuses every one's mind on the main task of pupils' attainment and the quality of their educational experiences. If there were no EDP – the government's strategy for school improvement and raising standards would be considerably weaker: the support and challenge to the 24,000 schools to set targets raise standards and improve would be diffuse and, the accountability and quality assurance would lack rigour. The LEAs would be deprived of a powerful plan of action to successfully implement their statutory duty to 'promote high standards'.

It is sometimes uncomfortable for both LEAs and schools in that poverty is now not an excuse for poor attainment but a reason for targeting improvement. That resourcing and teacher recruitment are a major context but not a reason for not focusing work of schools to how we make a difference. If the opportunity to sustain the role of the EDP within the government standards agenda is lost then the education of pupils will be the poorer.

It is the plan which will ensure both school, LEA and DfEE accountability for keeping standards at the heart of education as increasingly schools become self managing. It crucially places pupils, teaching, learning and professional development at the centre of the educational debate. However, as recently quoted by Professor Michael Barber: 'When the results of our students match the passions of our pronouncements, we shall know that we have kept our promise' (*American Educator*).

Interlude

Patrice Canavan
Headteacher, Sion Manning
Royal Borough of Kensington and Chelsea
RC Girls School

Sion Manning is an 11–16 Girls Catholic School with over 600 students. It became a beacon school in January 2000.

Effective LEAs 'make a difference'

The OfSTED inspection of Kensington and Chelsea made the judgement that 'the LEA's ten year campaign to improve its schools has been outstandingly well managed'. As headteacher of a beacon school in the LEA I am acutely aware that sustained success is hard to achieve, especially in the current educational climate which is very fast moving. The Royal Borough has many significant strengths, four of which have made a direct impact upon my own leadership namely:

1 support and challenge
2 comprehensive performance data
3 sustained levels of resourcing
4 a high quality professional development centre for teachers which is at the cutting edge of thinking and change.

1 Support and Challenge

This has been achieved in various ways, but principally through the role of the Link Inspector.

The role of the Link Inspector has been critical in supporting the drive to raise standards at Sion Manning RC Girls School. Each school in the Royal Borough has its own Link Inspector, and my Link Inspector has been with me since I became head of the school in September 1995. Together we have planned performance reviews, worked closely on staffing and teased out the many issues surrounding the controversial issue of performance management. Termly reviews were planned to marry the needs of our School Improvement Plan as well as, deliver LEA directives from central government. Our Link Inspector has willingly been guided by myself to carry out reviews relevant to the current needs of our school. Following these reports are issued which are always clear, focused and challenging.

The Link Inspector has also played an important role in supporting with us the setting of realistic and challenging targets. In particular conversations have centred upon the analysis and importance of prior key stage data and 'in-house' data produced by our own monitoring systems. The role therefore of the Link Inspector is well received, improving the quality of teaching, learning and standards. A Link Inspector who is competent, experienced and well briefed can make a real difference to a school, as my Link Inspector does at Sion Manning.

2 Comprehensive Performance Data

The Royal Borough has comprehensive data on all its schools which makes possible a statistical analysis of the achievements of the pupils since 1990. Data produced by the Research and Statistics Department at the Royal Borough is exemplary.

All headteachers receive quality documentation which provides a wide range of varying data, including pupil mobility, free school meals, fluency in English, teacher recruitment and retention, and a detailed analysis of public examinations. Headteachers do not provide information for the Research and Statistics Department, it is collated by the department and sent to headteachers in an easy to understand format. The 'value-added' data is particularly useful.

3 Sustained levels of resourcing

Since its inception in 1990, Kensington and Chelsea has put a high priority on education. It has always spent well above education Standard Spending Assessment (SSA). There have never been cuts in real terms in school budgets and all of the 1999/2000 increase in education SSA was passed on to the education budget. In the past two years the LEA had provided the large increases in matched funding for the Standards Fund. The headteachers have always felt that the generous and sustained funding by the Royal Borough has without any shadow of a doubt played a critical part in the raising and maintaining standards.

4 Isaac Newton Professional Development Centre for teachers

The above centre has been supporting teachers for ten years. During these ten years it has become one of the most prestigious centre in London. Under its principal it takes the professional development of teachers very seriously indeed and the development and the networking of good practice.

The centre itself is one of excellence and this is immediately apparent as soon as you walk through the doors. Its professionally smart appearance, its 'organised atmosphere' and attention to detail, including the student's display work, is an invitation to the willing learner to take this profession of ours very seriously. Under the guidance and leadership of its principal we are all encouraged to learn more about our roles as teachers and learners, future leaders and innovators. This centre quite simply enthuses encouragement and hope. The Primary/Secondary Professional Development handbook produced by the principal for teachers who work in Kensington and Chelsea and beyond, is the epitome of the high standards reflected throughout the LEA. The principal herself is a model professional who serves the profession well and values teachers of all abilities and strengths.

In conclusion I would say that the LEA has made significant difference to me as headteacher and many of my colleagues in the Royal Borough. I have tried to give a mere snapshot of this, in an LEA which is clearly one of the leading LEAs in the country as confirmed by its OfSTED report.

It is time to share good practice and enable others who may need extra support to also make that difference. With encouragement and support they can and will.

4 Dealing with schools causing concern

Martyn Cribb

A serious debate about failure is, in fact a precondition of success, 'Success for All' and 'Zero Tolerance of Failure' turn out to be synonymous.
Michael Barber, *The Learning Game* (1996)

Introduction

The identification of schools' strengths and weaknesses has been a responsibility many LEAs took on board at an early stage in their existence. In some LEAs there was a rigorous cycle of inspections and internal to specific LEAs there were procedures agreed with schools. The introduction of OfSTED inspections from September 1993 meant that for the first time there was a national system of inspection for all schools, agreed criteria, time scales and procedures for reporting to all the partners concerned. This was the first time that any country in the world had set out to monitor and evaluate the standards and the progress that schools were making. The impact has been profound not only on schools but also on the LEAs of which they are a key partner.

The development of the policy for identifying weakness and failure

Government policy is focused on individual schools rather than individual pupils. Since 1992 successive governments have adopted a robust approach to the identification and improvement of schools causing concern. The justification for this policy is that the pupils in the schools are being given a poor-quality education when they require a good education to prepare them for adulthood and the opportunity to enjoy their childhood to the full. The government's strategy identifies the individual school rather than the pupil, LEA or the nation and this ensures that support is focused on the cause of the problem which in policy terms is the school.

The 1992 Education Act established the responsibility for OfSTED to inspect all schools in England, and OHMCI for Wales has a similar responsibility. This was rapidly followed by the 1993 Education Act which set out the responsibility for the Registered Inspector to state whether or not the school was failing to provide a satisfactory standard of education for the pupils. This caused much concern in the early days and still does in some quarters. However, by the end of 2000 about 1,200 schools had been placed in special measures – approximately 3 per cent of primary schools, 3 per cent of secondary schools, 8 per cent of special schools and 6 per cent of pupils referral units, although the current 'live' figure is less than 400 schools. The reasons for school failure are summed up in a number of places but importantly the criteria for identifying a school as failing has been transparent since 1993. This marks the first occasion that the reasons for stating a school is underperforming and failing have been made known prior to an inspection occurring.

The regime of special measures has been followed up by the creation of a further category– those with serious weaknesses. These are schools that, although they are not 'failing to provide their pupils with an acceptable standard of education', do have a weakness in one or more critical areas of school life. This system was established by HMI from January 1994. It became apparent at an early stage in OfSTED's inspection regime that some schools were underperforming but had not been identified as requiring special measures. This led to a series of follow-up inspections by HMI to judge whether or not the pupils were receiving an acceptable standard of education. HMCI and through his powers HMI had been given the power to inspect any school or class of schools. These inspections were not designed or intended to check up on the judgements of the registered inspectors and their teams, but rather to ensure that pupils' education was safeguarded. Unions and some LEAs were deeply sceptical of these inspections. How could three or four HMI for one or two days produce a report failing a school when a whole inspection team, in some cases less than a year earlier had not reached that judgement? It is not possible to generalise but there may be cases where the registered inspector was less rigorous than required and the well-known rigour of HMI came to the fore. In some cases the school's performance had declined.

Since September 1997 registered inspectors conducting Section 10 inspections have been required to state whether or not schools have serious weaknesses. This ensured that schools 'found to have serious weaknesses ... cannot say any longer that they did not realise they were in this category' (*The Annual Report of Her Majesty's Chief Inspector for Schools*, 1997/8). It also ensured that the LEA knew and was in a position to take appropriate action. This extension of the categorisation of schools brought significantly more schools into the causing-concern net.

The introduction of the concept of schools causing concern and the powers for the LEA to intervene to tackle weaknesses if the school would not or could not was a further strengthening of the LEAs' powers to intervene (Education Act 1997). This new power enabled LEAs to take action where there was evidence to show that the school was not addressing weaknesses adequately. Importantly, many LEAs took the opportunity to allow schools to self-identify that they required support. This recognition of a school's ability to evaluate its own strengths and weaknesses and to seek help was a sign of LEAs' and schools' increasing maturity to identify and deal with problems.

The categorisation of schools into special measures or serious weakness means that perhaps 10–12 per cent of all schools have one or more aspects that give cause for concern. This is over 2,000 schools and the number of pupils affected could be as high as 1 million. This staggering number is being addressed but at the point when it appeared the numbers were reducing there are indications that changes to OfSTED's Framework for the Inspection of Schools introduced in January 2000 are increasing the rigour of the inspection regime and the numbers are rising again. In his annual report for 1999/2000 HMCI states that the picture is very mixed. Although 238 schools were removed from special measures, '230 failed their second inspection' and this '. . . is a cause for concern'. The challenge for LEAs is to make sure schools make progress and do not end up requiring special measures.

One event that shaped opinion was the so-called 'naming and shaming' of schools in special measures which were deemed to be making too slow progress. The naming of about a dozen schools was greeted with dismay when it occurred in the summer of 1997. The impact was one of shock and in some cases paralysis followed by concerted action. The policy adopted, however, had the desired effect of ensuring that the new government's tough new regime was taken seriously. Many LEAs reacted immediately and introduced new systems to ensure that the intervention did not happen to 'their' schools.

A further development in the category of schools causing concern is the introduction of 'underachieving schools'. This refers to any school whose 'performance is below that expected of schools in similar circumstances' (*Inspecting Schools: the framework*, OfSTED, effective from January 2000). This is likely to have the impact of challenging those schools which are not doing as well as they should and will challenge such schools to do better. Some LEAs including Tower Hamlets and the City of York 'encouraged schools to decide if they need to place themselves in the "schools experiencing difficulties" category' (Adding Value to School Improvement, the Education Network, 2000).

Power with responsibility for LEAs

Central to the role of the LEA is the improvement of schools. If the LEA's advisory/inspection service is doing anything that is not about school improvement it must be questioned whether the LEA has correctly identified its priorities. LEAs now have the responsibility to make sure that the priorities of central government are put in place and at the same time ensure that the will of locally democratically elected councillors is also implemented. The result can be a fine balancing act for senior officers. Persuading councillors that the requirement to address the government's priorities is at least as important as their local initiatives can be difficult. The reality is that there appears to be a broad consensus that the need to raise standards is crucial. At the same time many councillors with their fingers on the local pulse are very aware that raising standards and addressing local needs go hand in hand.

At a time when LEAs were worried that their powers were being eroded, the government was providing them with specific powers to deal with failing and seriously weak schools. These include:

- withdrawing the delegated budget;
- appointing additional governors; and
- preparing an action plan setting out the LEA's programme of support.

The SSFA 1998 gave LEAs similar powers to deal with seriously weak schools as failing schools. These powers enable LEAs to focus attention on the weaknesses and ensure that appropriate programmes were put in place, usually with the agreement of the school and the governing body but on occasion without their consent.

The Education Development Plan and schools causing concern

The Education Development Plan (EDP) was introduced for all LEAs with effect from April 1999. LEAs were required to prepare plans which for a three-year period detailed the programme of school improvement the LEA intended to put in place for its schools. A key priority for LEAs was to set out a policy for identifying and supporting schools causing concern. The term 'schools causing concern' was introduced as a concept at the same time as the EDP. It is a general term covering schools in special measures, schools with serious weaknesses and schools identified by the LEA which require support.

A number of LEAs, such as Lambeth, had already embarked on the road of setting out their three- or five-year programme for raising standards in schools and this included a statement recognising that it was necessary to address the issue of failing schools.

However, although since 1993 schools had been identified as requiring special measures and since 1997 as having serious weaknesses, few LEAs had produced strategy statements setting out how schools would be supported. Little had been done to codify how schools would be identified and then supported. Even so the introduction of the requirement to have a strategic statement for schools causing concern in all EDPs was accompanied by considerable debate. Not because the idea was not sound but because it was a matter of whether each LEA should have a statement for schools causing concern or one of the priorities should be for this. It was decided that all LEAs should prepare a strategic statement setting out how they would identify and intervene in a school causing concern. Those LEAs with a large proportion of schools causing concern were also advised by the DfEE to have a particular priority to address this issue.

The majority of statements for schools causing concern focused on how to provide sufficient support and at the same time ensure that all schools had sufficient time from the LEA's advisory services. It was common to find that the LEAs had set out a menu of support for schools causing concern on the basis of a set number of days. This enabled the LEAs to identify the cost of general support and monitoring for all schools and at the same time provided a rough guide to the amount of time needed to support schools causing concern.

Stoke LEA's EDP for schools causing concern (an example)

Stoke on Trent LEA has a detailed plan for addressing the needs of schools causing concern. However, the Education Development Plan states very clearly that: 'The ... (school improvement) programme is rooted in the inescapable logic that schools, not LEAs, teach children. Ultimately they must be responsible for improving themselves.' Importantly, the LEA has made very clear to schools the triggers that are being used to categorise schools and hence channel support. These triggers are based on OfSTED's framework for the inspection of schools. The following are the categories of schools now used by the LEA:

- improving schools;
- aspects of schools causing concern (including underachieving schools);
- schools causing concern;
- schools with serious weaknesses; and
- schools requiring special measures.

The identification of schools is based on a rigorous analysis of the performance of schools and 'The identification of schools by the LEA will be by one or more of the following routes:

- the annual cycle of school self-review and evaluation as previously outlined;
- the analysis of end-of-key-stage data, in particular comparison with evidence of performance trends and benchmark data for similar schools; and
- the collection and analysis of information at half-termly meetings of all senior staff, within the Education Department who have frequent contact with schools. The composition of the group will be the Director, the Senior Management Team, all heads of sections and all members of the Advisory Team.'

Another good example is that of Nottingham City which identifies policy and procedures, specific criteria for categorising schools causing concern and specific procedures to be followed in each of the four categories (EMIE Document, September 1999).

The *Code of Practice for LEA–School Relations* (now being revised) says very little on the amount of time that LEAs should spend in their schools although the Code is based on the concept of intervention in inverse proportion to success. There is specific mention of the need to agree targets for each school. Here the Code states 'the LEA should discuss with the governing body ... the targets set'. It goes on to state that 'the LEA should use its time and resources selectively to focus on those schools which need most help'. This reflects the government's determination to make LEAs work with schools in inverse proportion to success. In addition 'school visits should not be treated as the LEA's main mechanism for monitoring the performance of schools'.

There is an increasing number of systems for accumulating cross-LEA information which enables officers and advisers to understand what is happening to a school's performance. Essex LEA uses an electronic alert system triggered by the systematic analysis of data. A system devised in Warwickshire and now marketed commercially enables the LEA and schools to set out statistical information in diagrammatic form to show trends and patterns of performance. Use of pupil-level data is critical to this work and helps schools and the LEA to identify the performance of particular groups. However, schools need assistance to make sure that this information is used well. One headteacher in 1996 stated that 'It is all very well giving me this data but at the moment my LEA is not assisting me to use the data'. This is less of a problem now that the LEAs have got used to using data and many are well placed to present data in an easy to use fashion which enables the headteachers and the governors to interpret progress. The school profile for Lambeth is a good example of a well-presented set of statistics which benefits from the use of charts rather than tables of figures.

LEAs continue to use various patterns of time for school support, which are differentiated for schools causing concern. In Tower Hamlets, for example, there is a well-defined structure which has been agreed with headteachers and is a priority for the LEA's school development team. The broad pattern of time allocation is as follows:

- all schools up to 3 days per year;
- any school with a specific difficulty an extra 3 days per year;
- school causing concern 7 days extra per year;
- school with serious weakness 10 days extra per year; and
- school subject to special measures up to 20 days per year.

These are broad guidelines but provide the context within which the link adviser and the school can plan the support. Clearly, if a school requires more support, then this will be made available, but it may come from the use of independent consultants.

The role of the LEA

The role of the LEA is now clearer than for some considerable time especially in the area of schools causing concern. The Audit Commission put forward a number of models for LEAs and emphasised the strength of the partnership model where LEAs work with schools and empower them to provide the quality education to which pupils are entitled.

The key role for any LEA with underperforming schools is to:

- identify weaknesses and failure;
- locate and address the causes of the weakness;
- empower the schools and the governors to tackle the weaknesses;
- put in place robust measures to prevent further failure.

LEAs are becoming increasingly proactive in the search for strengths and weaknesses in schools. In the early 1990s as LEAs became more involved with OfSTED inspections the capacity to cope with the weaknesses of schools was reduced in some circumstances. By the turn of the century, many LEAs were reducing their commitment to OfSTED to ensure there was enough time to support schools. Hampshire LEA had found that the cost of redemption was even more time consuming than inspection. As a result the LEA has progressively restructured itself to embrace a more school improvement-oriented strategy (reported in D. Fisher, *Partnership in Progress*, NFER).

One central issue for LEAs and for schools is that finding that there is a weakness in school performance is one thing but identifying the cause of the weakness in performance is another. The action plan is the tool for identifying what needs to be done but prior to that there is an analytical stage which should expose the cause of the weakness. The best written OfSTED inspection reports provide a very good analysis of the causes of the weakness but for the LEA there may be no recent OfSTED report and it is necessary to carry out the analysis themselves. This analysis of the situation as opposed to description should take all the information available and come to a judgement about what is the cause of the weakness. Arthur Andersen Consultants refer to this as 'situational analysis' and this is a useful term for describing the process of identifying why something is not working.

Identifying a weakness in a school is a key skill not only for the link adviser but also for all the LEA staff. The head of an LEA's catering service reported that the 'behaviour of the pupils was largely uncontrolled by the teachers and this spills over into mealtime which resembles a bear garden'. This unfortunate comment is one that usefully describes the non-educationalists view of pupils' behaviour in one school. Indeed, it is one that most people can associate with and reflects the common perception of what some failing schools are like.

This illustration serves to show how important it is for the LEA to garner information from a wide range of sources. Cross-directorate information flow is critical to detect the strengths, weaknesses and the movements in the effectiveness of schools as soon as they begin to occur.

The triggers for intervention need to be set out clearly and precisely so that there is transparency for all. Schools need to know what to expect and the LEA must be able to state what the schools will receive in the way of challenge and support.

> Sometimes statistical trends take heads by surprise. The headteacher of a school when told that the statistical indicators showed that the performance of her school was declining was amazed. Two LEA advisers took her through the evidence and convinced her that there was a problem she and the staff needed to confront. After the initial shock her reaction was that but for their 'intervention I think the school would have been in serious trouble with OfSTED. Thankfully for the children in particular the LEA helped and challenged us to get things right'.

Making Headway, published by OfSTED in 1998, reports on some of the effective ways of how headteachers from good schools have been used to support other schools in difficulties. The ideas of mentoring, replacing headteachers, pairing, using agencies are now well known. The value of using experienced and able headteachers to support others is well documented and the in-depth knowledge of HMI is illustrated by the many examples given. But for many LEAs the issue is ensuring that moving a headteacher from one school will not lead to destabilizing another school and making matters worse.

Headteachers often take the lead in asking for support but on occasion they find it difficult to continue the process of improvement. In this case study the headteacher recognises the need to tackle low achievement but is concerned about the LEA recognising the school as one that is causing concern.

> **One form entry primary school experiencing difficulties**
> The headteacher of a primary school had been in post for less than six months and was worried about the quality of teaching and the low standards. However, the headteacher had been active in the establishment of the aims and vision for the school and was in a good position to move on to tackling the quality of teaching.
>
> The link adviser shared the headteacher's view about the schools and together the headteacher and the link adviser agreed a plan of action for the review of teaching. This involved convincing the headteacher that it was her role to monitor the performance of teachers and that the involvement of the LEA should be seen in a positive light, one that was intended to help the school and speed up the process of improvement.

Bowling Community School was placed in special measures by HMI when they returned to assess the progress that the school had made since the OfSTED inspection. Progress was slow and one of the reasons for this was the poor quality of teaching. The headteacher with the aid of a retired HMI and senior managers reviewed the quality of teaching in the school and found that there were many weaknesses. In too many lessons the pupils, many of whom had poor reading skills, were being expected to carry out tasks that they could not do, did not understand, or which were unclear. All the teachers were stating the aim of the lesson but were not making it clear what had to be done. It proved very difficult to convince staff that there was a problem. The answer came when it was decided that all staff should have the opportunity to observe lessons. Teachers were coming out of lessons and stating that 'it was half way through the lesson before I understood what was to be done'. What hope for the pupils who were struggling with the work from the outset? But it was from this point onwards that teachers appreciated the need to ensure that the purpose of the lesson was clear, that pupils knew what they would learn in the lesson and how they would know if they had learnt it.

In this same school the LEA inspectors were carrying out the standard monitoring role but teachers were sceptical of the inspectors' ability to identify accurately the levels of ability of the pupils and what support they required. To overcome this the headteacher asked the inspectors to teach some model lessons. To their credit the inspectors took on the challenge and were able to produce good-quality lessons and help the school's staff to plan and deliver lesson more effectively. This work is a major challenge for LEA inspectors but one that they must take on. They have the experience and should be prepared to use their knowledge and expertise to tackle some more difficult schools. It may be that the LEA advisers and inspectors would benefit from working in the classroom with pupils to keep their skills up to date. In the same way some of the very good teachers – Advanced Skills Teachers – can be used to support other schools.

Intervention by the LEA

Intervention by the LEA is likely to be most effective if the school accepts there is a problem and agrees with the LEA's programme of action. It is important for the LEA to be open about the process and have well-documented and agreed procedures for informing the school that the LEA is worried about its progress, based on the *Code of Practice on LEA–School Relations*.

Placing additional governors on a governing body is a regular occurrence when schools are placed in special measures. Often the additional governors are there to ensure that good practice is developed rather than adding specific skills. However, on occasion it is necessary to place a significant number of additional governors to ensure that a chair is appointed who will lead the governors effectively. However, where there is a 'flooding' of a governing body there has usually been resistance and progress to improve the school has suffered. One of the key features of OfSTED's publication *From Failure to Success* (1997) was the key part played by the governors to raise standards. Only one of the case studies is headed 'Governors', but it is important to note that in six out of the eight case studies governors are quoted as playing a significant part in the improvement of the school.

The removal of a school's delegated budget ensures that the LEA not only has control of the budget but it also means that the LEA has control of the personnel powers. This may be very important in a school where restructuring may lead to a number of redundancies. However, it is important that the governors continue to be involved in the budget-setting process to ensure that they do not lose sight of what is to be achieved. The Code of Practice has swept away the practice of a few LEAs to remove the delegated budget as soon as a school is placed in special measures. It is now essential that the budget is only removed where there is evidence that this is the appropriate course of action to take.

Many LEAs now use some form of strategy group to work with a school causing concern to ensure the support and challenge is pitched at the right level. Lambeth called them School Improvement Groups and Tower Hamlets calls them Targeted Intervention Groups but they serve the same purpose – that of supporting and challenging the school to improve. The groups comprise the link adviser, headteacher and chair of governors and will draw in other people as required. Targets can be set and people tasked with particular things to do. It is a working group clearly focused on the need to improve the quality of education. Most of the LEAs have the groups chaired by the LEA's link adviser. This provides a good link to the other LEA services which can be drawn in to lever up standards. In both the LEAs mentioned each school group reports regularly to the Director of Education.

In 1999 the Beacon Council scheme was launched and one of the themes identified in the scheme was 'Helping to raise standards by tackling school failure'. From all the submissions, visits and presentations which ultimately saw the awards of beacon council status to Suffolk, Camden, Blackburn and Darwen and North Tyneside LEAs the key characteristics were identified as follows:

- a culture of high achievement;
- high-level strategic and operational support for governors;
- sophisticated systems for the collection and analysis of performance data;
- high-calibre link advisers;
- effective systems to monitor school progress;
- early warning triggers;

- prompt intervention where schools are vulnerable;
- tackling issues of access from a school improvement perspective;
- ways of sharing good practice;
- where schools fail, ensuring effective interventions that have impact;
- promoting headteachers' capacity and capability; and
- providing LEA leadership from the top.

In terms of ensuring effective interventions that have impact where schools fail, the report highlights a number of strategies:

- take determined, decisive action;
- use objective audit of current performance as a starting point;
- help schools to engage parents and the local community in the recovery strategy;
- ensure cohesive support from across the directorate or through external provision;
- build on the expertise of best teachers in the school;
- provide a rigorous challenge to the chair of governors and the headteacher but, where appropriate, be sensitive to the need for counselling;
- develop effective community links and partnerships to challenge rumour;
- focus on teacher development;
- consider but choose carefully from the full range of support strategies (e.g. ASTs, seconded headteacher, mentoring and peer coaching);
- maintain a strong focus on monitoring; and
- celebrate progress and success.

Addressing specific difficulties

Most LEAs now have satisfactory ways of addressing and identifying schools' needs. In some schools the problems are not whole school and may be limited to a curriculum area such as English or it may be an aspect of the school such as attendance. In most cases where there is one issue others are lurking close by. However, it is important to ensure that the one weakness is addressed so that the school can avoid other difficulties arising. In Tower Hamlets as in other LEAs the Strategic Statement for schools causing concern contains a category of schools which have specific weaknesses. These are schools where the school or the link adviser has identified that one or more aspects of the quality of education are not satisfactory. The identification of such a situation triggers time and resources from the LEA to support the school to tackle the weakness.

A number of LEAs in the Excellence in Cities programme are working together to identify Beacon Departments. This scheme is similar to the Beacon Schools but is intended to enable LEAs and schools to identify the most successful and effective departments in the LEA. The intention is that these 'model' departments will be able to support other departments to improve. This will add to the pool of knowledge about good in-service training (INSET) and training providers. It may also be the source evidence of best practice which will add to the collective pool of information about good management and teaching in schools and provide a further resource in supporting schools causing concern.

Life after special measures and serious weaknesses

The progress from special measures, serious weaknesses or specific difficulties to health is not one to be taken lightly. Sir Geoffrey Hampton, former headteacher of Northicote School in Wolverhampton has stated on a number of occasions that 'the most challenging management task I ever faced in schools was the period after Northicote School came out of special measures'. This was because of the challenge of keeping the school going and ensuring that the progress made was built on and progress was maintained. It is probable that all schools require some continued support after the inspection that states they are back to health. In some LEAs this takes the form of extended support from the link adviser such as double time in the first year, or elsewhere a mentoring scheme for the headteacher to keep the school moving.

Many LEAs are still uneasy about central government dictating the terms of the debate. Of especial concern was, and still is, the control being put on finances, but in the case of schools causing concern Standards Fund money was being targeted at those schools where the need to raise standards was the greatest. This was the first time that money was being provided for those schools who needed it.

Working in partnership

'Headteachers need never feel alone!' states OfSTED (*From Failure to Success*, 1997). In its publication it outlines a number of ways in which headteachers can be supported. This includes the use of consultants and other headteachers to support the headteachers who have to cope with what is an arduous role. In one LEA a very experienced and successful headteacher was engaged to work with the headteacher appointed to a school causing the authority concern. The mentor headteacher was known to be a very good trainer and had the skills to help the new headteacher tackle many of the issues which she lacked experience of tackling and in some cases lacked the expertise. This proved to be a fruitful relationship and although the school is still experiencing difficulties good progress is being made. LEAs need to identify the headteachers who make good mentors and trainers in order to support weaker schools. This can have the benefit of enriching the career of the mentor headteacher and providing a very real stimulus and value for the community of schools. Not all head-teachers can be used in this role and it is for careful negotiation to see what is the best way forward.

One of the features of headship often spoken about is the loneliness. This is especially true for the headteachers of schools in special measures. Trying to support the headteachers of schools in special measures is essential but few LEAs have managed to create an environment where the headteachers of schools in difficulties are themselves supported. In 1998 Hertfordshire LEA working in conjunction with some neighbouring LEAs and with the support of an adviser from the Standards and Effectiveness Unit at the DfEE ran a one-day meeting for the heads of up to 30 schools in special measures. This successfully started a pattern of support for the headteachers which continues to operate. One headteacher at the first conference stated that 'It is good to meet other professionals who are in the same position and discuss ways of improving my school'.

Making strategic partnerships with consultants and other specialists in the field of school improvement is essential if the LEA is to have the capacity on tap to tackle difficulties when they arise. Many LEAs do not have the specialists to provide the support for schools in difficulty. Strategic partnership with a group of consultants can provide LEAs with the skills base to be able to tackle weaknesses in schools.

In Lambeth in 1997 there were eight schools in special measures. Most of these schools had a key issue concerning the improvement to the quality of teaching. The LEA did not have the capacity to provide teacher coaches to support the staff so worked in conjunction with a group of consultants to provide the necessary support. Experienced headteachers who were also OfSTED trained inspectors were used to coach teachers. The OfSTED skills were essential to enable the coaches to identify the strengths and weaknesses of the staff and to help them identify the way ahead. Once the support needed was identified the coaches were able to work in the classrooms with staff and tackle some of the poor practices. The result of this work was impressive and all the schools were able to improve their perfomance markedly.

Capacity building

The LEA's role to support schools causing concern is well defined and written about in many places, but it is essential that the LEA staff know the most effective ways of keeping up to date. In 1999 the Standards and Effectiveness Unit worked with three Universities and the Virtual Staff College to develop a training course for LEA advisers. These were based on the competencies being developed by the Virtual Staff College and the National Association for Education Advisers, Inspectors and Education

Consultants (NAEAIC). The purpose of the course was to identify the skills and abilities of an LEA team and then prepare a training course which built on these attributes and built towards the competencies. A number of these courses have been run. One course run with Warrington LEA included headteachers and LEA officers as well as advisers. To some extent this indicates the movement of LEAs away from a single focus on advisers delivering all the LEA support for school improvement to one where all the LEA staff are involved.

Further capacity can be built into the LEA by the use of headteachers. Some LEAs have used headteachers for a number of years as advisory heads. This has worked well but some headteachers are particularly skilled in specialist areas. LEAs should be identifying headteachers who are good leaders and managers and able to support other schools.

> The headteacher of a very successful inner-city primary school had been in post for 10 years. She had no wish to leave but was looking for another challenge and approached the Deputy Director to discuss the possibility of work with other schools. The headteacher had already worked informally with one new headteacher and this provided a very good opportunity to formalize this arrangement and make a payment to the school to enable the headteacher to buy in some support when she was out of school supporting other colleagues.
>
> This system worked well and when another headteacher needed support it was possible to identify very quickly who to use.

For this system to work it is essential for the LEA to:

- know its headteachers well;
- provide some training for the headteachers who will be supporting others;
- monitor the impact of the work to ensure that the planned outcomes are met; and
- identify the funding to support headteachers coming out of school.

Working in partnership with headteachers provides LEAs and all schools with increased capacity and skills to tackle difficult situations. Recently in the *Times Educational Supplement* there was an advertisement for a headteacher to work in a challenging inner-city boys school which is in serious weaknesses. There was an enhanced salary and the opportunity to work with the LEA in an advisory capacity for one day per week when the school had been turned round. This creative use of posts in schools is likely to give some headteachers an added challenge and refresh their interest to carry on working in schools and support others at the same time.

The government's Beacon Schools Scheme provides the opportunity to identify, celebrate and use the skills of some of our most successful schools. This is already bearing fruit and it is possible to extend this further. Professor John Gray has suggested that rather than pairing the very good with the very weak it may be as, and perhaps more, useful to pair weak schools with schools which are a little better and improving. The crucial point here is that the better school is still improving. Also essential is the need for the headteacher of the 'better' school to be a good headteacher and able to support the headteacher of the weaker school.

The use of information technology provides another important means of developing the capacity of LEAs to improve schools causing concern. The Standards and Effectiveness Unit's CD ROM 'School Securing the Future' is an interactive training package focusing on the most effective ways of turning round failing schools.[1] There are a number of case studies and issues which are illustrated with use of video clips and text from OfSTED reports. The CD contains an hour's worth of video and can be used individually or with audiences of governors or teachers.

The building of LEA's capacity to improve schools is essential if the LEA is to survive. Intervention in LEAs and the outsourcing of underperforming LEA services is common in LEAs that OfSTED find to be ineffective. It is likely that the smallest LEAs are most vulnerable because they do not have the range of skills and abilities even though the number of schools to work with is commensurately larger. Part of this capacity building is likely to revolve around strategic alliances with independent partners. This is likely to be most effective in the area of schools causing concern where LEAs will be searching for consultants with the skills to challenge and support schools. To be effective LEAs must evolve and adopt new working practices to ensure that the focus is firmly on raising standards of the weakest and lowest performing schools.

Summary

Removing failure from the education system is the responsibility of all those engaged in the delivery and monitoring of the system. LEAs have a central responsibility to identify and help turn round schools causing concern. This is a major task in some LEAs and one that the DfEE and OfSTED believe requires support from outside the LEA. However, it remains to be seen whether the intervention into LEAs will work or whether it will be more effective to work in strategic partnership to tackle failure.

There are a number of things that the LEA should do to improve the rapport with schools and remove failure:

- Work in partnership with schools to create shared understanding of the LEA's role.

- Work precisely and decisively.
- Ensure that there is a wide base of knowledge about the skills available inside the LEA.
- Ensure that all in the LEA, including schools, realise that the success of education in their authority rests largely in their hands.

Even the best run LEA may have schools that run into difficulty. It is essential that LEAs have the capacity to tackle school weaknesses. For this they must have sufficient resources and the proper direction to be able to support and challenge their schools.

---

[1] *Schools Securing the Future* is available from SEU.

5 Promoting and disseminating good practice – 20 strategies

David Woods

An effective LEA will work with the DfEE and other LEAs to celebrate and spread best practice.

(*Excellence in Schools*, DfEE, 1997)

Make sure you catch people doing something well.

(Charles Handy)

Only connect . . .

(E.M. Forster, *Howards End*)

Disseminating good practice is one of the eight national priorities for school improvement as set out in the EDP Guidance for LEAs and schools. Its importance is stressed in most school improvement literature and in DfEE publications such as *Excellence in Schools* (1997) and *Raising Aspirations in the 21st Century* (2000). It needs to be done well at different levels and points within the education system and there needs to be an appropriate synergy and interaction between schools, LEAs, the DfEE and national agencies such as OfSTED, QCA, the Teacher Training Agency (TTA) and the General Teachers Council (see Figure 5.1). Individual schools will want to maximise their capacity to share their own good practice within their organisations whilst needing to develop connections to that of other schools, their LEA and to the DfEE and other agencies to gain a wider perspective and increased professional knowledge. Similarly individual LEAs will want to develop their internal capacity to develop and disseminate good practice with their school communities and with national government.

LEAs, schools, and teachers need to:

- manage their knowledge better;
- create some new professional knowledge about teaching and learning;
- find ways of transferring or disseminating their knowledge and skills more effectively.

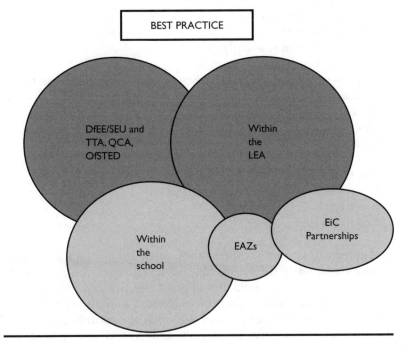

Figure 5.1 Best practice

Defining terms

In the literature of school improvement the terms 'best', 'good' and 'innovative' practice are used in a variety of ways and it is important to be clear at the outset about the use of these terms.

- *Good practice*, which is the more universal term, is used generally to mean practice which is professionally judged to be effective but may require further evidence and validation.
- *Best practice* is used, particularly by the Standards and Effectiveness Unit (SEU) and DfEE literature to mean practice which is proven over time and can be backed up by supporting evidence.
- *Innovative practice* may highlight new and interesting ways of doing things with no more than early indicators of success in a particular context.

All of these types of practice have a part to play in the quest for continuous professional development and school improvement but the absolute standards for 'best practice' are that it

- should lead to the raising of standards

- can be applied in various settings
- is sustainable over time
- has been validated externally.

For the purpose of this chapter, however, we will generally use the term 'good practice' but indicate differences as appropriate. Whether practice is defined as 'best', 'good', or 'innovative', there are a set of common questions for schools, LEAs and national bodies in its development and dissemination:

- How to identify?
- How to 'Kitemark' and assure quality?
- How to connect?
- How to develop further?

This chapter will set out in context the contributions of national government and particularly the Standards and Effectiveness Unit at the DfEE to the identification and spreading of good practice and links to schools and LEAs, and the contribution of individual schools with their links to LEAs, but mainly it will concentrate upon the contribution of LEAs. LEAs are the hinges between schools and central government and a major player in other key partnerships that seek to disseminate good practice to raise standards, such as Education Action Zones and Excellence in Cities Partnerships. LEAs are in a good position to act as researchers, developers, brokers, connecters and facilitators of good practice and by doing so they can add significant value to school improvement.

One of the aims of the Standards and Effectiveness Unit is to support LEAs and schools by publishing and disseminating effectively what works in raising standards. It does that principally through the following strategies:

- Developing and promoting the Standards Site which has a growing number of platforms ranging from schemes of work for teachers to examples of effective LEA practice and also has interactive areas which enable teachers to share good practice with one another, keep abreast of new developments including research and have access to information in teaching resources and training and development.
- Building a best practice database through monitoring LEA EDPs, LEA OfSTED inspection reports, beacon council bids, reports on beacon and specialist schools, evaluating the literacy and numeracy strategies, and reviewing EAZs and EiC partnerships.
- Supporting weak and failing schools – for example the development of a CD-ROM 'Connect for Better Schools' and the associated training programme for LEA advisers.

- Various publications on key aspects of best practice, for example *From Targets to Action* (DfEE, 1997) and *Building Professional Knowledge* (DfEE, 2000), a collection of LEA case studies.
- Working with the Standards Task Force sub-group on case studies of best practice.

Alongside this, QCA are developing good practice models of curriculum and assessment, the TTA is developing materials on pedagogy and standards for school leadership and OfSTED is using its extensive inspection database to write reports across the whole spectrum of school improvement and good practice.

Similarly, working in partnership with LEAs and other stakeholders, the DfEE is establishing a diversity of education provision so that good practice and the resources that are generated with it can benefit those in other schools and the wider community. David Blunkett in a speech to the Social Market Foundation on Transforming Secondary Education (15 March 2000) stressed that 'we need to establish an excellent and diverse education system where schools work together; where schools learn from each another; where good practice and ideas are shared rapidly; where pupils are a part of a wider learning community'.

This is being done principally through the specialist school programme (1000 schools to be established by 2003 and 1500 by 2006) across a range of specialisms and the beacon school programme which will rise to 1,000 schools by 2002. The latter are schools of recognised excellence that are funded to work with other schools to share good practice. Within the Excellence in Cities Partnerships LEAs and schools share good practice and decide how resources are allocated to develop learning mentors, learning support units, learning centres and small EAZs, beacon and specialist schools and clusters for gifted and talented provision. Excellence in Cities provides the capacity for each school to build on its own success and then share this with others. Further the 73 Education Action Zones with groups of schools ranging from 12 to 30 working together have a prime purpose in developing together innovative and good practice to raise standards of achievement, alongside Excellence Clusters and up to 100 small zones.

Throughout the country individual schools are attempting to build their own professional knowledge and internal capacity to develop good practice – a process described by David Hargreaves in his DEMOS pamphlet on 'Creative Professionalism: the role of the teacher in the knowledge society' (1998) as having several steps:

Step 1   Generating ideas: sowing
Step 2   Supporting ideas: germinating
Step 3   Selecting the most promising ideas: thinning
Step 4   Developing ideas – shaping knowledge and practice
Step 5   Disseminating knowledge: sharing and practice

To do this effectively schools have to build and develop teaching and learning cultures through induction, continuous professional development, collaborative planning and assessment, coaching and mentoring, collective review, researching the evidence and finding ways to share good practice. This will have to be done both inside and outside the school, and here the LEA can play a critical role in stimulating the debate, nurturing ideas and making the necessary connections to add value to school improvement. Indeed the Hargreaves model works just the same way for LEAs as for schools. LEAs and schools can work together profitably to:

- establish school self-evaluation processes to identify good practice;
- establish action research programmes to develop good practice;
- use expert practitioners as coaches and mentors;
- develop quality circles to nurture and feedback practice;
- collect and publish examples of good practice;
- connect to higher education institutions to promote better teaching and learning;
- contribute to local intranets and the DfEE standards site;
- extend the capacity for leadership and management of schools.

In all this, partnership and co-operation is key and as expressed in 'The Code of Practice'

> All schools need to keep in touch with the development of best practice, and benefit from the challenge of a regular infusion of fresh ideas. All need access to a range of support services from outside. All, and particularly the most successful, can contribute to sharing and celebrating excellence. The principle of partnership is not limited to relations between LEAs and schools. It also applies to schools working with other local schools . . . and to LEAs working with local governors associations and many others as part of their local leadership and networking function.

There is no better way to demonstrate the strength of the partnership than by seeing skilled professionals of all levels in the LEA working together and sharing good practice to raise standards of achievement.

The rest of this chapter sets out in detail some twenty strategies whereby LEAs can build professional knowledge and promote and disseminate good practice mostly with their own school communities but also with each other and in partnership with national government.

Twenty LEA strategies to promote and disseminate good practice

1 An agreed policy statement to promote and disseminate good practice

Although this is not a requirement of the Education Development Plan, effective LEAs are setting out in that document or an appendix a strategic statement to pull together the development and sharing of good practice across the education community of schools and stakeholders. They have also consulted widely on this policy and in this sense the LEA is being proactive and acting as a change agent and catalyst for school improvement and is therefore positively seeking to make a difference to what schools do to raise standards. Such a policy statement would need to set out the following:

- a process of partnership and collaborative working which is open and transparent;
- the use of particular datasets and evidence to identify good practice;
- a mapping of networks and identification of 'hubs and spokes';
- a research and development strategy;
- partnership with other agencies outside the LEA in promoting and disseminating good practice – the SEU, TTA, QCA, OfSTED, the General Teachers Council (GTC) and HEI;
- links to established agencies and partnerships inside the LEA also committed to sharing good practice – e.g. Education Business Partnerships, Early Years Development Partnerships, Excellence in Cities Partnerships, Education Action Zones;
- a publications and communications strategy which might include a local intranet; and
- a commitment to developing school and LEA self-evaluation which would result in better action planning to support the identification and promotion of good practice.

2 LEA register of expert practitioners

Expert practitioners may be defined as those who have credibility with practitioners, have the capacity to coach others, and who are 'leading edge' professionals whose work has been externally validated. Obvious examples can be taken from the National Literacy Strategy, which has local expert teachers, or the National Numeracy Strategy, which has local leading maths teachers. The LEA co-ordinators for literacy and numeracy should be able to make sure that teachers have a chance to observe these expert teachers at work and learn from their practice. Similarly a register of advanced skills teachers in the LEA who have one day a week to work with other teachers and schools and some negotiation with them as to where and when they can be used to best effect in the LEA would be exceptionally useful. Many LEAs still retain advisory teachers, some on a seconded or part-time release from schools, whose services are purchased by schools and who therefore have to demonstrate value for money. These expert practitioners are skilled change agents working across the curriculum and bringing together groups of teachers and schools to compare and improve practice.

However, an LEA could go further than this by identifying and verifying expert practitioners who are in the schools as a resource for others to visit and learn from. These may be teachers of early years, special needs, English as an additional language, specific subjects or expert learning assistants. What unites them is an expertise that gets beyond teacher talk and the sharing of ideas, to the specific enhancement of skills. An effective LEA should know where its best practitioners are and work with schools to make the best use of them.

'Good schools and good LEAs grow good teachers.'

3 LEA-approved 'centres of excellence'

Beacon and specialist schools have already been referred to and there will be comments later on the LEA role in their networking, but LEA centres of excellence would complement this provision by establishing LEA beacons in order to celebrate success at a wider level. These local centres of excellence are likely to be a part or aspect of a school's provision which has been acknowledged by OfSTED and local LEA review processes with perhaps other quality marks, to be excellent and can be kitemarked as such by the LEA for a maximum of three years before having to be reassessed. These could be primary schools with outstanding early years provision perhaps linked to Surestart or schools with excellent special needs provision, or personal and social education or community development, or art and music. Most commonly 'approved' by LEAs currently are primary schools with excellent literacy and/or numeracy and ICT practices or secondary subject departments whose practices are deemed to be advanced and worth observing at first hand. These parts of the school are likely to have:

- clear policies and strategies;
- successful practices and achievements backed by evidence;
- rigorous monitoring systems for practices;
- regular review of practices in the light of evidence;
- changes to practices/policies as a result of evaluation; and
- they could offer valuable professional development for other groups of teachers.

The identification and communication of these 'centres of excellence' by the LEA would make a considerable difference to opportunities for professional development and the enhancement of skills to raise standards.

Schools who, either through self-evaluation and data analysis or OfSTED reports, have particular weaknesses in their provision would now have a range of opportunities to study at first hand, in similar schools, how to improve their practice. A good example in Staffordshire Schools' Networking Project which publicises a range of opportunities for interested staff to attend sessions in particular schools.

4 Using associate heads and deputies as coaches and mentors

A previous strategy referred to the use of expert teachers to promote and disseminate good practice and this section refers to the use of expert leaders and managers of schools to do the same. Most LEAs have management development programmes often linked to Headlamp, the National Professional Qualification for Headteachers (NPQH) and the Leadership Programme for Serving Heads (LPSH) and to the National College of School Leadership, but effective LEAs have gone beyond this and have identified their best heads and deputies which can be used, subject to governors' approval and the immediate needs of their own schools to act as mentors and coaches for other schools. In the spirit of openness and transparency that best befit a professional community, senior managers of schools can be invited to apply for an associate adviser position which would normally be for a short term secondment or perhaps the equivalent of one day a week. Having identified and appointed this cohort of people the LEA is in a much stronger position to deploy relevant, credible expertise to other schools to improve practice. LEAs have often used this technique to support weak and failing schools in which case heads and deputies have been seconded full time for significant periods but the enlistment of heads and deputies as associates even for limited periods adds a considerable resource to the capacity of an LEA to spread best practice and improve schools.

5 'Name and Acclaim' series of publications

One effective strategy to disseminate good practice is to produce a series of publications on particular themes based on case studies of good practice in schools. This serves two purposes – recognising valuing and celebrating good practice in individual schools and giving other schools access to that good practice. Effective LEAs will produce a calendar of internal publications on chosen themes and invite schools to supply case studies. These case studies will have to be verified possibly by using the link or curriculum adviser or OfSTED evidence but brought together in one publication they provide a considerable boost to particular topics.

For example Warwickshire LEA produces a termly 'Name and Acclaim' series. The same technique can be used on a subject specific basis through the use of termly or twice yearly newsletter or bulletins to schools to identify and celebrate good curriculum practice in schools: something that is widely used in Staffordshire LEA amongst others.

Occasionally anthologies of ideas in school improvement collected from schools are published, such as Birmingham LEA's *Butterfly Book* (1997) which describes the small changes schools have introduced which have produced considerable differences with reference to chaos theory and the concept of the 'butterfly effect'. Hillingdon LEA has a 'Have You Heard' series of publications for identifying and disseminating good practice which brings together local, national and sometimes international data and ideas and Suffolk LEA has its house magazine entitled *LEArning*.

6 Research projects and publications for schools including training videos

On a different level to the collection of practical ideas and case studies from individual schools is the development of LEA research publications. These are often the product of LEA established working groups which are brought together for a set purpose usually to investigate a particular issue or concern. Here expert practitioners from schools work together with LEA Advisers and officers, sometimes with assistance from HEI, to produce materials that would be of value to all the education community. The choice of subject may well arise out of the set EDP Priorities for improvement where the audit has shown particular weaknesses in present provision and performance such as Key Stage 2/3 transition, boys' achievement, ICT-assisted teaching and learning.

Some LEAs have gone further, following the example of TTA and QCA in particular, and have produced training videos on particular issues linked to a publication or guidance notes. Often these new research publications and videos are launched at an LEA conference which concentrates energy and attention on the particular subject under scrutiny and helps to ensure that these good practice materials reach the right audience so that they can be put to practical use very quickly. There are a tremendous range of examples across the 150 LEAs in England and some have made a national impact as well as a local impact because of the quality of their ideas, for example Shropshire's target setting and use of data publications written by Keith Hedger in collaboration with David Jesson at Sheffield University and the Kirkless materials on raising boys' achievement. The TTA have also funded school-based research partnerships to make systematic use of research findings as a means of enhancing teaching and learning and there are good examples in Northumberland, Manchester and Norfolk LEAs amongst others.

7 LEA INSET provision and development opportunities

Under Fair Funding LEAs have more than ever to consider carefully the range and nature of INSET provision to schools. They are obviously not a monopoly provider and schools now have a good choice of INSET provision from a variety of services. Clearly 'best value' is the watchword since most INSET has to be paid directly from school budgets. LEAs are allowed to retain some funds for school improvement which matches activities set out in the EDP and they will use this to make a strategic difference to the raising of standards of achievement and in particular to network and disseminate good practice. This may take the form of providing courses and conferences, maintaining 'school improvement' centres as part of teachers' centres with centrally held resources and access to the most sophisticated data sets. Often expert practitioners are brought to work together on a commissioned project or short courses which can effectively communicate the best local and national practice in a given field. For example some LEAs have identified particular curriculum areas where they have offered specific support and leadership to schools. Northumberland LEA and Hammersmith and Fulham LEA (in partnership with HEI) are using knowledge and materials from research into thinking skills as a focus for the development of teaching strategies. All secondary schools in Hammersmith and Fulham are involved in the Cognitive Acceleration through Science Education (CASE) and Maths Education (CAME) projects in collaboration with King's College, and the CASE project has now been extended to ten Primary Schools.

Some far-sighted LEAs organise series of 'breakthrough' seminars for all interested parties to attend. These are intended to bring the best national and sometimes international speakers to spark and stimulate debate and discussion and to kickstart educational change. Similarly, other LEAs will organise conferences open to participants from all over the country with high-profile experts and presenters to connect an issue of national importance and to showcase the best practice available. Recent examples include conferences on thinking skills, social inclusion, and accelerated learning.

8 Twinning Schools

It is now a requirement for new beacon schools to twin with other schools, often outside the LEA, to share and disseminate good practice. Excellence in Cities partnerships also provide the means, particularly for like secondary schools, to twin across partnerships and compare practices and policies for such common issues as teaching and learning for gifted and talented pupils, the best practice of learning mentors and learning support units as well as other practices. However, effective LEAs can add to this provision by constructing their own twinning arrangements so that the benefits of good practice can be directly exchanged.

The most common form of twinning is related to a 'successful' school linking with an 'unsuccessful' school, particularly a school that has been deemed to either be in need of special measures, or have serious weaknesses, or be underachieving or generally causing concern to the LEA.

Great care needs to be taken with matching such schools and ideally they will be reasonably close 'statistical neighbours' with the successful school able to offer good practice and practical solutions for improvement in a given context. Of course it also needs to be borne in mind that the less successful school will also have something to offer in the partnership.

However, there is also a great deal to be gained in twinning, as equal partners with both schools able to offer different strengths and good practice to the other. Such activities as joint INSET days, shared working groups, peer observation of teaching, twinning subject departments in secondary schools, bringing key postholders together, such as literacy and numeracy co-ordinators and special education needs co-ordinators (SENCO), and work-shadowing, will enhance the capacity of both schools to improve, although the size of the LEA and the possible difficulties over competition will need to be taken into account.

9 Benchmarking with family groups of schools

Family groups is the name commonly given in LEAs to groups of similar schools based upon such indicators as:

- the percentage of free school meals;
- the percentage of pupils with English as an additional language;
- the percentage of pupils with special educational needs;
- the level of pupil mobility; and
- school size.

Facilitated by the LEA such groups of schools are encouraged to compare their PANDAs and their assessment outcomes, particularly related to literacy and numeracy in the primary school and subject performance in the secondary school but also attendance and exclusions. The provision of first class data by the LEA is essential and these meetings are another way of increasing the data fluency of schools and of teachers. This in turn leads to the identification of value-added or 'trend-busting' schools and the identification of these factors in teaching and learning and school organisation that make a real difference to pupil achievement and may lead in some cases to more ambitious target setting. Such family groups can share expertise across a wide range of policies and practices which leads to further opportunities to visit like schools to observe teaching and learning, to match post holders and to work together on common challenges. For example Blackburn with Darwen have developed Benchmarking Learning Groups for Headteachers, where each termly session is followed by 'homework' involving collaborative work with another head.

The LEA plays an important role in such groups as an enabler, facilitator and in the provision of key, comparative data but the real ownership of educational change and improvement lies with the schools themselves.

Charles Handy in his book *Beyond Certainty: the Changing World of Organisations* (1996), refers to benchmarking as the discipline of measuring yourself against best practice in any functions or field, and remarks that this technique 'ought to be an ingrained habit – to aim to be not just good enough but as good as can be, to look beyond oneself, to shun complacency and the false comforts of talking only to people like oneself'. The same discipline of course applies to LEAs as organisations as we will see in a later section.

10 Good practice in school self-evaluation and the use of local quality frameworks

Many LEAs through their Education Development Plans have done a great deal to facilitate and develop school self-evaluation often building upon the OfSTED Inspection Framework for Schools and the OfSTED/SEU publication entitled *School Evaluation Matters* (1998). In particular they have developed their own quality frameworks or benchmarks so that schools can test out the quality of their provision. This helps to develop 'shared language' within an LEA around quality thresholds, good practice and continuous school improvement. As an example of this, Essex LEA has developed a quality framework which covers twelve dimensions: the entire range of a school's activities. From learning and achievement to pupil support and welfare, key objectives are matched with a range of success indicators. A second level to the framework helps schools to identify and analyse the types of evidence by which they can measure, whether the success indicators have been achieved. Somerset LEA operate a similar quality framework.

Hampshire LEA has produced a 'barometer' or analytical tool to measure departmental effectiveness in secondary schools which is now used in schools and by advisers in review activities. In Salford LEA school reviews are conducted jointly by advisers and senior managers against a set framework so that senior managers can be trained in self-evaluation as well as the means to improve their school.

11 Networking beacon and specialist schools and early excellence centres

All LEAs now have beacon and specialist schools and these are set to increase significantly by 2003. Effective LEAs have an important part to play in helping to network these schools and joining up the map with other local centres of excellence so that hubs and spokes can be clearly identified.

> [W]here schools share good practice, tackle common problems and offer specialist opportunities to pupils at a range of schools, each school can help to enhance performance across an area – creating networks of excellence that go beyond a single school.
>
> (David Blunkett, *Transforming Secondary Education*, 2000)

This applies particularly to specialist schools and even more so for LEAs who are part of Excellence in Cities partnerships as they have a role in nominating these schools. Facilitating connections and links to help these schools spread their expertise appropriately is something that LEAs should be directly engaged in if they want to secure maximum benefit for other schools and make sure that good practice is disseminated to the best effect. For example Gateshead LEA has made sure that all its specialist schools are twinned with other secondary schools in the LEA as well as linked with local primary schools.

Similarly, as beacon schools are funded to work with other schools to share good practice, LEAs should work in partnership with them to make sure they can have a maximum impact on other teachers and schools. They can offer a wide and varied range of activities as the means to disseminate their practices and with the LEA acting in a brokerage role the potential needs of partner institutions can be better matched to the strengths and services operated by the beacon schools. Examples include seminars for teachers from other schools, mentoring, work-shadowing, the provision of INSET training, demonstration lessons, the release of 'teacher consultants' to other schools and the preparation of curriculum planning material. An NFER evaluation of the pilot beacon schools in 1999 recommended that LEAs should foster a general climate for schools of sharing with and learning from each other, identifying and connecting up the different initiatives, facilitate the acquisition by teachers of the 'cognitive and interactive skills' which are the major dimensions of learning about teaching and find ways of using the Beacon idea to manage the tension between intervention in inverse proportion to success and the entitlement of all schools for support and challenge for school improvement.

On a much smaller scale some LEAs have been able to work profitably with the twenty-nine approved early excellence centres which have been established to show how care and education can be integrated to provide services for children aged from 0 to 5 that are open all day and throughout the year. They all provide local beacons of excellence for early years providers and early years partnerships.

12 *Quality Circles/Networking Practitioner Groups*

In a recent NFER Report on *The LEA Contribution to School Improvement* (July 2000) nine out of ten LEAs studied cited networking groups as a major catalyst for sharing good practice. According to this report this was also the strategy most likely to be mentioned by the teachers in schools who appreciated the opportunity to come together on a regular basis with colleagues outside their own schools. The models most often quoted were LEA curriculum panel meetings and school cluster configurations. Depending on the size and the capacity of the LEA to some extent one would expect an effective LEA to be able to bring together and facilitate the following groups of practitioners:

- Newly qualified teachers
- Heads of department
- Special educational needs co-ordinators
- Deputies (phase groups)
- Headteachers (phase groups)
- Subject teachers
- Literacy and numeracy co-ordinators
- Early years co-ordinators
- Gifted and talented co-ordinators (EiC)
- Learning mentors (EiC)
- Chairs of governors

In terms of disseminating good practice dynamic groups of practitioners who are carrying out very similar tasks in schools day after day have an excellent opportunity to add value to the whole process. As with all group meetings carefully structured agendas and innovative activities are necessary to generate a real focus on school improvement and raising standards and here the LEA has a key role in facilitation. The gains of having these regular groups can be immense both in terms of personal professional growth and the dissemination of good practice. Such groups can often organise exhibitions of good practice hosted by particular schools or LEA centres and become a powerful force for celebration and professional growth.

> Good professionals are engaged in a journey of self improvement, always ready to reflect on their own practice in the light of other approaches and to contribute to the development of others by sharing their best practice and insights.
>
> (*Professional Development*, DfEE, 2000)

13 Establish a Research and Development Forum to promote good practice

The establishment of such a forum would signal the vital importance of identifying, developing and disseminating good practice in the professional community of the LEA and give this activity the central direction it requires. Clearly an LEA should always work with its schools to promote and develop a research culture and that would bring many benefits in developing bottom up change but there needs to be some means of driving forward the development, commissioning and communication of such good work.

The learning organisation should mean two things – an organisation that learns and an organisation which encourages learning in its people.

(Charles Handy, *The Age of Unreason*, 1995)

Setting up a Research and Development Forum would need careful consideration of the following factors:

- Membership – the need to draw in all sections of the professional community.
- External links – particularly to local HEI provision but also to government bodies such as the TTA and QCA.
- The commissioning of research – presumably this would be based on a careful analysis of performance data and other evidence.
- The organisation of 'breakthrough' seminars and conferences to highlight research findings and spread good practice.
- Disseminating outcomes on a regular basis through practitioner groups, publications and the use of ICT.
- Working with the DfEE to promote best practice research scholarships and professional bursaries.

14 *Partnerships with higher education institutions (HEI)*

A very valuable resource to any LEA wishing to be positively involved in innovation, research and good practice would be a partnership or partnerships with HEI. Some LEAs are fortunate in having several universities or colleges within their boundaries whilst others need to seek out new partners. Partnerships can work at different levels:

- Local teachers undertaking further qualifications such as MA or M.Ed. but who are able to do much of the research as a school-based project.
- Teaching practice students who may undertake small-scale studies to investigate good practice.
- As a reciprocal arrangement for HEI using local schools for teacher training purposes. HEI staff could contract to provide some seminars and workshops.
- Participation in the LEA's Research and Development Forum.
- Universities/colleges hosting major conferences and exhibitions to promote and share good practice.
- Helping to establish new training schools (starting September 2000) with higher education or a teacher-training provider partner. Such training schools will explore new approaches, carry out and use teaching research, and share the results of their experience and examples of good practice.

- Assisting with best practice research scholarships particularly in EiC areas, where teachers undertake small scale research and disseminate their findings. The programme includes support for each teacher through a mentor with a proven track record in research.

There are already many good examples of LEAs and HEI working profitably together on professional development and promoting good practice. The University of Cambridge and Hertfordshire LEA have established a Learning Partnership to design new approaches to professional development with heads, teachers, LEA advisers and University staff engaged collectively in school based research and development with a shared set of levers for improving teaching and learning. Essex LEA uses HEI partners to ensure that outcomes of school improvement initiatives are rigorously monitored, evaluated and reported often in published journals, conference papers or book form.

15 Local intranets – good practice websites

We have already noted the importance of the DfEE Standards Site in disseminating good practice across the country and the National Grid for Learning represents a new opportunity to share information and materials and build networks between teachers and the Virtual Teachers Centre on the grid for the exchange of ideas and experiences. Some LEAs and EAZs have established their own intranets and websites to share teaching and learning materials and ideas and provide appropriate databases of good practice. Telford and Wrekin LEA as a new Unitary took the opportunity to set this system up from the start and has installed the UK's biggest e-learning facility in the schools with the first secure, high-speed broadband network and the largest school-based video conferencing facility in Europe. Telford and Wrekin's Grid for Learning enables both individual and whole class interactive tuition as well as the simultaneous broadcast of lessons from a central service to the areas 85 primary and secondary schools.

In Cheshire there is a curriculum intranet (IALT) supported by LEA-developed software which is available to all schools. Advisory days are allocated for training and quality control for curriculum and teaching submissions to the site and in Manchester there is a 'This worked for me' website.

16 Promoting Quality Standards

There are a range of Quality Standards that schools and LEAs can work towards. The Investors in People standard focused on improving people performance to improve the organisation's performance. Some LEAs have entered into partnerships with their local TEC to develop Investors in

People (IIP), with joint TEC/LEA/Schools Steering Groups. All partici-
pating schools are assured of external support from colleagues trained as
IIP advisers and assessors and negotiate particular forms of support to suit
their own needs. Banks of resources are available and workshops and professional development sessions enable staff from different schools to come
together to share ideas and practice.

Other LEAs have worked closely with the Basic Skills Agency to
promote the achievement of Quality Marks in Literacy and Numeracy,
and there are other examples of LEAs and schools using the Business
Excellence Model.

17 Working with LEA statistical neighbours and twinning LEAs

Just as effective LEAs are directly assisting schools to improve by facilitating
and organising 'family groups' of schools to work together and share good
practice and also twinning particular schools so LEAs need to look to their
own improvement by working with their statistical neighbours or even direct
twinning. All LEAs receive from OfSTED annual profiles (the equivalent of
PANDAs) which as well as giving them a fix on their collective performance
compares their standards with those of their statistical neighbours. This can
give a valuable impetus to seeking improvement and sharing practice
particularly from those LEAs in the group who seem to be performing least
well. Similarly an analysis of LEA OfSTED inspection reports can indicate
where the best practice can be found, always allowing for the particular
context. Although the preferred pattern for LEA groupings is still through
geographical clusters, which can of course still promote good practice, some
LEAs are beginning to organise contacts or meetings with statistical neighbours as well on particular issues or themes. There are also some interesting
cases of twinning – for example Nottingham City LEA and Blackburn and
Darwen LEA, both new unitaries and statistical neighbours. They have compared good practice in turning round weak and failing schools, the use of
performance data and target setting. In cities Birmingham and Sheffield have
established a link to compare their work in Excellence in Cities developments but also to run joint conferences for headteachers.

18 Sharing case studies

At the heart of school improvement is the building of professional knowledge and if LEAs are to make a real contribution to helping schools raise
standards they need to be proactive about finding out what is working well
elsewhere in terms of providing the best services directly to schools or
'brokering' services for schools. Good networking already exists through the
Association of Chief Education Officers (ACEO), the Society of Education
Officers (SEO), the Society of Chief Inspectors and Advisers (SCIA) and the
National Association of Inspectors and Advisers in Education (NAIEAC).

The Local Government Association (LGA) through its Education Network has produced a number of good practice publications, in particular, *What Makes a Good LEA?* (ed. Martin Rogers, The Education Network, 2000). LEAs have now got their own platform on the Standards Site and this will be an excellent medium for sharing case studies of good practice. The Standards and Effectiveness Unit at the DfEE has published a pamphlet on *Building Professional Knowledge* (2000), which contains 15 case studies that are also available on the Standards Site. Clearly there is a rich collection of innovative, good and best practice materials and practices in the 150 LEAs both in terms of improving LEAs and improving schools. The challenge is for every LEA to promote this good practice both internally and externally. A good approach to this would be the holding of LEA 'open days' where particular practices and processes could be explained and discussed.

19 LEA school improvement 'butterflies'

The modern study of chaos theory tell us that tiny differences in input can quickly become overwhelming differences in output. In weather, for example, this translates to the butterfly effect – the motion that a butterfly stirring the air today in Beijing can transform storm systems next month in New York. We can learn from this that very small initiatives taken by LEAs and schools can have a disproportionate effect as a catalyst for school improvement. LEAs could collect together these small initiatives and disseminate them. Here are three examples.

1 LEA advisers asked the primary schools to pick out an aspect or aspects of their work that they believed to be demonstrating good practice and every month one school was asked to host a twilight session which was open to all interested parties. This provided teachers and others with an informal opportunity to walk around the school, talk to colleagues about the particular feature of good practice and look at the resources employed. For the second half of the session, the teachers gathered together for a presentation by the host school with an opportunity to ask further questions. These meetings have been very well attended and proved to be an excellent means of disseminating good practice.

2 New headteachers were asked by the LEA to host visits to their school by other new heads. The first part of the visit was given over to a tour of the school where the heads were asked to specifically observe aspects of the learning environment. The second part was a collective discussion, facilitated by an adviser, on the quality of the learning environment observed with ideas and suggestions for improvement. New heads have gained a good deal from this particularly as being new in post they were not sensitive to criticism and anxious to get good ideas for improvement.

3   The LEA had established a working group of professionals on developing effective teaching and learning culture in schools. One of their major recommendations was that weekly staff meetings in primary and special schools should be held in classrooms rather than the library or staffroom. Every teacher, with a classroom assistant if appropriate, would host a staff meeting on a rota basis and the first item on the agenda would be an explanation of the particular learning environment and how the classroom was organised. This collective review process has helped everybody both to celebrate good practice and to improve against their previous best. Some secondary schools have adapted this approach and have asked subject departments to host staff meetings again with the idea of departmental staff explaining the learning environment to their colleagues and particular teaching and learning strategies.

20 *Networking with beacon councils*

There are beacon schools and we have suggested in this chapter the development of local centres of excellence and there is now a Beacon Council Scheme which aims to identify centres of excellence in local government from which others can learn. One theme identified in 1999 was 'Helping to Raise Standards by Tackling School Failure' and the scheme invited councils to apply for beacon council status through providing evidence of their work in this area.

As previously referred to in Chapter 4, four councils were granted beacon status – and there have been several 'roadshows' to share and develop further this particular aspect of LEA good practice.

The Beacon Council Report of the Findings in November 1999 included a section on 'Ways of Sharing Good Practice' which is worth quoting in full.

Ways of Sharing Good Practice

- families of schools and benchmarking with the best;
- register of validated good practice and emerging good practice;
- use school expertise at all levels to inform and develop policy and to provide professional support and challenge;
- establish policy for best practice dissemination which not only promotes but also ensures conditions to enable transformation and change are in place;
- evidence based research and development to identify and share best practice in secondary school departments;
- provide highly focused training and development programmes;
- encourage a culture of ongoing teachers' professional development;
- use link advisers to provide brokerage.

In 2000 there was 'support for underachieving groups' which has helped again in the dissemination of good practice between councils and LEAs.

Summary

We have seen that in the promotion and dissemination of good practice all sectors of the education system have their part to play but that LEAs are particularly well placed to join up all the various players and demonstrate that the collective sum of the schools' efforts within the LEA are greater than the individual parts. They thus have a major role in *connecting* good practice whether this be through quality circles, family groups, consortia and clusters, specific working groups, the provision of databases and registers of expert practitioners and centres of excellence, twinning schools or local intranets. Before connecting there needs to be *identification* of good practice which relies mainly on the work of advisers and advisory teachers working with Associate Heads and teachers to observe practice in schools, to write reports, to participate in joint reviews and to examine other forms of evidence such as OfSTED reports and the achievement of quality standards. Once identified, good or innovative practice needs to be *quality assured* to make sure that this practice is best practice and does lead to the raising of standards, can be applied in various settings and is sustainable over time. This will demand that the LEA has some process of validation which will include the scrutiny of performance data over time, benchmarking and some methods of review beside working with other external agencies. Finally the effective LEA should be a *quality developer* and generator of good practice if it is to really make a difference to raising standards of achievement, as well as the quality of teaching and leadership and management. This will be a combination of establishing a Research and Development forum, using appropriate coaches and mentors, facilitating the production of research papers and publications, highly focused INSET programmes, good links with higher education and above all establishing a climate and a culture where professional development and school improvement can flourish. As a major part of this LEAs have to encourage, nurture, cherish and disseminate good practice wherever and whenever it occurs.

6 Strategic professional development

Stella Blackmore (with colleagues)

> Good professionals are engaged in a journey of self-improvement, always ready to reflect on their own practice in the light of other approaches and to contribute to the development of others by sharing their best practice and insights.
>
> David Blunkett, Foreword to *Professional Development* (DfEE, 2000)

Introduction

Professional development is a key function for an effective LEA working in partnership with its schools and is part of every Education Development Plan. There are many partners to consider in drawing up a strategy such as the DfEE, the Teacher Training Agency, the General Teaching Council, higher education institutions, subject associations and professional associations. LEAs need to demonstrate that they can both provide and broker support for teachers, heads and governors to assist them in their prime task of raising standards as well as train their own personnel including, in particular, advisers and inspectors. This chapter examines how one county LEA, Warwickshire, with some 250 schools, has set about the task.

Developing school leadership and management

Inspectors in Warwickshire each have a dual role as phase, subject or aspect specialists, and as a link with a patch of schools covering all phases. Each school has an entitlement to a basic link allocation of three days a year, of which there must be at least half a day in every term. The content of visits is determined in part by schools' priorities, though some elements are determined centrally and notified in advance; for instance, in the spring term of 2000, all primary schools were offered the opportunity to audit current curriculum provision against the requirements of Curriculum 2000 in order to ensure adequate preparation, and to identify support needs for individual institutions and on a county wide basis. The PSHE curriculum has also been the subject of debate, in line with our EDP which seeks to promote the integrity of holistic provision as an essential ingredient of promoting quality as well as high standards.

Each of the five areas of the county also has a named link Area Education Officer who provides first call support for a variety of management issues such as finance and personnel queries. Officers have a particular responsibility to work with governing bodies on headteacher appointments; they attend patch governors' meetings to brief governors on policy implementation and to mediate national requirements. One of the officers has the overall responsibility to manage the Governors' Unit, and to work closely with the Training Officer. Officers also offer a training package designed to audit strengths and weaknesses in governing bodies, and suggest areas for training and development which will enhance understanding of the governors' strategic role. We do not have the capacity to attend every governors' meeting, but attempt to monitor the quality of the headteacher's reports to governors, the attendance at meetings, whether a full complement of governors has been appointed to every school, and the quality of minutes. Extensive guidance, and a very comprehensive training programme support the governance role. In the few cases where delegation has been withdrawn, the officer concerned works in partnership with the school to remedy the weaknesses until such time as the governors are again able to assume financial responsibility for budget deployment.

In all matters to do with support for school leadership and management the LEA works closely with representatives of the diocesan bodies, who are involved with policy development, support for denominational schools causing concern, and the interpretation of the national agenda in such initiatives as Performance Management.

The link role provides an important forum for development activities; in our increasingly frenetic lives it seems to make sense to aim for 'best value' out of every activity. Perhaps one of the greatest challenges for headteachers and managers is to develop and implement a monitoring policy which is effective, manageable and achievable. As part of the EDP we have initiated an ongoing programme of paired observations with headteachers to support a moderated view of teaching quality, and the opportunity to take part in partnership activities such as work trawls and pupil pursuits. This seems to have been an enormously successful strategy; monitoring standards, content, presentation, National Curriculum compliance, consistency of application of school policy and curriculum coverage are now well embedded into many schools' monitoring arrangements. It is also clearly important to offer pupils the opportunity to be active partners in school development, and pupil pursuits are a time and cost effective strategy to gain a student's eye perspective on school ethos and environment. We have developed several useful schedules for use in these activities, and also promote and use those developed by schools; for example classroom observation schedules developed as a result of school based audits and policies for teaching and learning, from which school priorities are drawn, and which reflect the schools' aim statements.

The balance of inspector deployment across the county in terms of specialism has been carefully constructed to ensure that there is at least one primary phase specialist serving each area. These colleagues have responsibility not only for their own link schools, but also act as a 'first call' reference point for their area where additional phase specific expertise is required. This may entail corroboration of quality of teaching issues, support for solving management or class organisation problems, advising on building adaptations or curriculum advice. Primary schools are also able to request up to one half day a term from a specialist subject inspector to replace a half day of link activity if this better meets their immediate need.

Raising the quality of teaching

In Warwickshire we firmly believe that the primary function of the LEA is to secure school improvement, and that this process takes place in schools. Fundamentally, the arena for change is in classrooms; this is why the emphasis on raising standards should focus on the interaction between teachers and learners. Schools are expected to operate within a framework of autonomy. Though successful schools will be led by strong managers, improvements in standards can only be assured through skilled teaching by competent, well-motivated staff.

A variety of benchmarking data is used to complement OfSTED and our own inspectors' findings relating to teaching quality. Wherever possible we try to maximise the impact of any initiative by employing different strategies simultaneously. For example, our LEA Profile, while showing a significant improvement in the performance of the lowest attaining and achieving schools (which we like to attribute to the consistent implementation of a 'robust' intervention policy) appears to show that we are less successful in raising 'good' schools to the 'very good' category. Why should this be? The Profile clearly identifies low teacher expectation as a significant contributory factor, and this is a fairly consistent finding throughout the phases. In order to combat this we are ensuring a sharp focus on improving this aspect of teaching quality by linking a range of initiatives:

- making all schools aware of the issue of low expectations through meetings and link visits, especially where this is pertinent to the performance of individual schools;
- analysing and exploring on a one to one basis any low PANDA grades;
- ensuring that in every lesson observation undertaken by our own Inspectors that there is an explicit judgement on teacher expectation and the impact on standards which is fed back to the teacher, head, and logged on a note of visit;
- undertaking a survey on the use and impact of county guidelines on provision for gifted and more able pupils, and encouraging attendance at county network meetings;

- including positive role models of high expectation as an explicit aspect of Beacon school application and provision, particularly in areas of socio-economic deprivation;
- providing exemplar materials, for instance high-quality marking as an aid to pupils' self evaluation and target setting in order to raise esteem and confidence and promote high aspirations in pupils themselves;
- providing training for governors on their role in monitoring the quality of teaching; and
- promoting a variety of strategies for supported school self-review to help identify areas for development within a structured framework.

It is also important to make sure that within the democratic process elected members have the opportunity to foster a breadth of understanding about both the reality and the rhetoric of education in a day-to-day school context. The structure in Warwickshire includes cross-party Policy Advisory Groups (PAG) whose function is to debate policy issues before making recommendations to the Cabinet, which has a corporate decision making function, and which includes a portfolio holder for Education. The Chief Inspector is the lead officer serving the School Improvement PAG, and elected members are keen to understand the implications of the OfSTED framework in determining quality, how judgements are made against the criteria, and crucially, the indicators of all categories defining teaching quality. Most elected members also serve as school governors, and are thus well placed to influence schools at local level, as well as in strategic budget decision making as county councillors.

Another strand of the EDP is specifically designed to raise awareness of a range of issues bearing directly or indirectly on teaching quality. Throughout the year the county publishes a series of documents under the title 'Raising the Profile'. These are intended to promote a better understanding of the strengths and weaknesses within the LEA profile, while the content of each pack can be used at individual school level with staff, parents and governors to support the dissemination of national initiatives and statutory requirements or priorities within a school development plan. Consistent features of the format include suggestions for discussion, reference material, exemplar policies or processes and overhead projector texts. Already published in the series 'Raising the Profile' are 'Homework' and 'Primary Curriculum 2000'. Good practice is identified and disseminated through our 'Name and Acclaim' series. The 'Name and Acclaim' series are collections of school case studies on successful strategies for school improvement which take a particular theme every term. For example:

- spring, 1999 – focus on literacy
- summer, 1999 – focus on target setting
- autumn, 1999 – working with parents
- spring, 2000 – extra-curricular activities

The Management Development Programme

The framework for the Management Development Programme in Warwickshire is set out in a policy document which was consulted upon, agreed and now forms the basis of an EDP activity for the life of this current EDP. The annual content is devised and managed by four steering groups addressing the needs of primary headteachers, primary deputies, secondary headteachers and secondary senior managers. The groups meet in each half term with LEA officers to identify priorities for the coming year, develop a programme to meet the needs of the constituency groups and to contribute to the quality assurance of the programme.

The identification of the needs of senior managers in the area of 'management development' is based upon the following processes:

- an analysis of school OfSTED reports for the preceding year which can highlight common issues;
- an analysis of the LEA OfSTED report for county aspects of leadership and management;
- a comparison of benchmarking with LEA statistical neighbours;
- national priorities; and
- local aspects of concern elicited through personal contact with members of the steering groups or evaluations of the programme (which also contain a section allowing the identification of future needs).

Elements of the annual programme are designed to meet needs in different ways. A basic induction of two half-day sessions is provided in weeks three and four of the first term of appointment. This is for every new headteacher, new to headship, new to Warwickshire or appointed as an acting head. The sessions enable heads to meet colleagues from the LEA and from other schools informally. The content covers the basic services of, for example, human resource management, finance, property services, information technology and communications in the LEA, as well as some training in child protection. The process enables some initial networks to be established for mutual support.

Termly half-day entitlement modules often address an agreed theme by starting with the theoretical framework followed by a case study or two to disseminate good practice, finishing with a focused discussion to take forward the application in schools. For example, last year one of the Primary Headteachers' Entitlement Modules supported the work in schools to improve the 'quality of learning'. A professor from the University of Warwick led the thinking in the first part of the session, which is always repeated across the county to enable easier access. Two case studies followed, one school presenting its work with pupils on 'thinking skills' and how this contributes to improvements in learning. The other school shared their approaches to monitoring the quality of learning and how they evaluate their findings, leading to a further action plan for school improvement. Two themes taken up by secondary colleagues in the last year have been 'behaviour management' with input from the staff of the PRU, and 'developing middle managers', which has been followed up by a costed programme developed by our Education Development Service (EDS), the business unit managing professional development.

Each of the leadership groups plans an annual conference, with keynote speakers sharing their expertise, followed by a wide choice of seminars and workshops. These conferences are often opened or closed by the County Education Officer or Chief Inspector. In addition to providing high quality speakers at local venues and the opportunity for taking forward a related issue in a practical way, the conferences seek to facilitate networking. The mutual support engendered by this process cannot be underestimated in a climate of continual change. The opportunity to hear the Chiefs of Service is also designed to be supportive and continues to build the relationships between the LEA and schools upon which the School Improvement Agenda is predicated.

The Management Development Programme aims to decrease the sense of isolation and facilitate networking. Whilst recognising that school improvement is what happens in the classroom, it brings about a common agenda of issues to explore and disseminates good practice to support the development of all schools. The programme is well attended, for example with 96 per cent of all primary heads accessing at least part of the programme in the last academic year. Non-attendance can be followed up sensitively to ensure that no headteacher becomes isolated without access to school improvement matters. The cost effectiveness of the programme is evaluated and provides very good value for money. Clearly economies of scale are possible, and this, together with clear objectives and the partnership of the LEA, schools and others such as the University of Warwick, enables a balance of support and challenge in moving forward together on school improvement issues.

Case study: early years/Newman College

The national expansion of early education requires the LEA to provide teacher input to all the county's funded early years settings. Whilst there is a strong commitment within the county to high-quality early years education, historic funding limitations have meant that it has only a small maintained early years sector and a limited number of early years specialist teachers. There is, however, an extensive network of other early years settings, led in the majority of cases by able and committed nursery nurses, and a parallel range of nursery nurses employed by the LEA. Many of these colleagues are at the top of their grade and lack progression routes in their chosen field.

In order to address this and to provide the county with the early years specialists it needs the LEA has linked up with Newman College. Together we have developed a ladder of related qualifications, consisting of an Early Years Certificate in Higher Education, an Early Years Diploma in Higher Education and a BA in Early Years Studies, and an opportunity to achieve qualified teacher status. Study is part time and taught at the local teachers' centre on a day release and evening basis, with cover provided for LEA employees.

A high level of interest in the courses has been expressed, both locally and by neighbouring counties, and the quality of students accepted onto the programme has proved exceptional. The close link between theory and practice, which is fundamental to each of the courses, has meant that within the first year students are using their new knowledge and skills in their work with children.

Training inspectors

This section supports the development of a strategic plan to offer a continuing professional development programme for inspectors and Area Education Officers. Their role, in common with most education personnel, is constantly changing. Consequently, the emerging needs for the team and individuals must be met if they are to remain credible and effective. Given the pace of change recently, it may be an ideal time to re-visit the policy for CPD within the team of inspectors, which together with an audit of skills and competencies, will help to frame future developments in this area. The processes below are linked to specific skill or knowledge based competency development as examples of the types of professional development undertaken in this authority.

Induction is a vital component of CPD and starts with the period post-interview and before take-up of appointment. Familiarisation visits and pairing with a mentor are the starting points for effective induction, to ensure that the new colleague feels able to contribute to the work of the team in a short space of time. Induction is needed to the county, in terms of geography, personnel and committee structure; to the Department, in terms of an introduction to the work of different sections and business units; to the Section as an overall understanding of the core principles and purposes of the post held and finally to the role. The dual role of Specialist and Link Inspector demands much of the new appointee. The background and experience of the individual will usually have developed a strength in one of these areas more than another. As a consequence, the induction programme needs to be differentiated at this point and continues, in conjunction with mentoring, for the first year. All of the team undertake to provide support for each other in the sharing of expertise and the development of specific skills. For example, the Early Years Inspector is called upon to share her knowledge of good practice in this area and will plan a visit to a link school for a paired observation with another member of the team. Similarly, a paired visit to discuss target setting with a secondary headteacher may be called for as part of induction, for a colleague from a primary background. Termly evaluation of induction allows feedback to continually develop the process and supports early identification of further induction needs.

The policy for CPD supports the entitlement to on-going professional development and this is linked to the workplan, in the identification of time for this activity. Some of the training is undertaken by each individual. Specialist areas of knowledge need to be refreshed and updated and this often comes through specialist conferences and networks. There is the entitlement to OfSTED training and encouragement to undertake one or two inspections per year in order to better support schools in our understanding of the OfSTED process. Inspections also offer a means of gaining a greater insight into school improvement. Individuals continue the process of paired professional development started in induction, and negotiate with others to develop an aspect of their work. A professional development library is maintained to support individual reading; subscriptions are taken out to certain journals and the contents of these, and some books bought centrally, are circulated electronically to all team members. The library also offers a central resource for the dissemination of OfSTED, QCA, TTA and DfEE materials.

The opportunity for team training is limited, due to the demands on the team. However, in the meetings' plan for the year, care is taken to ensure that team training days are identified and this enables the team needs to be met in a cost-effective manner; often joint training days are planned with the teacher adviser team. Team training revisits the values and principles of the team and re-establishes core purposes in a changing climate. This itself highlights the need for the further development of some skills. For example, skills of data analysis and interpretation, together with the use of the CD-ROM 'Excellence in Warwickshire Schools' to provide case-study material, have been developed to support link and specialist roles. Whilst the Information Technology skills of the team vary across a spectrum found in any environment, there is always a will to improve these further. By planning small groups offering a range of applications such as 'Powerpoint', 'Advanced Use of Lotus Notes', with the use of spreadsheets or the exploration of specialist curriculum software, it is possible to meet the needs of individuals working in small teams. Briefings are formally timetabled half termly in order to offer the opportunity to disseminate material from conferences of interest to all, or to ensure that there is a vehicle for the sharing of key information that may need more time than a meeting or opportunity for clarification or debate. These have been used recently to explore the issues in the Green Paper and 'Performance Management' in particular.

Team members are encouraged to undertake further study, leading to additional qualifications where possible. The authority supports active links with the University of Warwick and through the Virtual Staff College, there are colleagues studying for further degrees. In order to plan for the most effective use of resources, and in particular the time element, it is important to draw together the needs of the individual and the team into an annual, costed plan. For this to happen, the process of needs identification has to be understood.

An individual's right to continuing professional development should include an annual appraisal of performance, which in turn facilitates the identification of further areas for development and an action plan to support these areas. The Schools' Team in Warwickshire is piloting appraisal against a competency framework for inspectors and Area Education Officers. As well as self-evaluation, feedback against these competencies is sought from three individuals (different colleagues each year), who have a knowledge of the appraisee at work. Two of the contributors are headteachers of link schools, whilst the third is from another context, and may be a governor, an individual from a LEA business unit or a member of the Schools' Team. The feedback is synthesised by the line manager of the appraisee for the annual appraisal. Areas for development can then be discussed and the appropriate training and development incorporated in the overall training plan. Termly meetings for review and development can then check progress against targets and the underpinning action plan.

The Schools' Team in Warwickshire, as in the corresponding structures in many other LEAs, is stretched in meeting the demands made upon it. The skills, knowledge and confidence of the team have constantly to be increased to meet these growing demands. A coherent commitment to the professional development of team members is a prerequisite of continually improving the understanding of and impact on school improvement. It is also a tangible reminder of the value of individuals to the effective working practices of an LEA.

Supporting newly qualified teachers

Strategic professional development starts with a commitment to newly qualified teachers. As entrants to the profession, they are not only the teachers bringing a fresh perspective and enthusiasm to the school improvement agenda of today, but are also the headteachers of tomorrow. NQTs, however, face challenging demands in the complex task of meeting the Induction Standards in their daily practice, in classrooms and cultures which may differ greatly from those encountered in Initial Teacher Training. Added to this, there is a very real stress of continual assessment, with a final outcome which dictates their future careers. Supporting NQTs as a strategic issue demands careful thought and attention to detail.

This LEA's induction programme is made up from the following elements:

- briefings for headteachers;
- briefings and newsletters for governors;
- training for induction tutors;
- written guidance to complement the information in DfEE Circular 5/99 and the TTA booklets; and
- induction programme for NQTs.

The task of supporting NQTs is a partnership between all of the parties above and the church authorities, in the case of church schools. For the partnership to be effective, it is important that there is clarity of roles and expectations. The quality assurance of the induction process has been consulted upon, agreed between the parties above and is set out in a LEA policy document.

There are clearly some statutory responsibilities for the 'Appropriate Body' in establishing a telephone contact for NQTs, for assessment and the maintenance of an effective database and for the appeals procedure. These constitute the minimum responsibilities of the LEA. In practice, it is the processes that underpin these, together with the quality of the interpersonal relationships between headteachers, induction tutors, LEA staff and the NQTs that impact on the effectiveness of support. The development of these relationships and the understanding of partnership as a concept, are addressed through much of the work of the Schools' Team,

Inspectors contribute to the induction support in the roles of Link Inspector, Specialist Inspector and Inspector for CPD. In common with most LEAs, the vast majority of the two hundred plus NQTs who join the authority each year, arrive at the start of the academic year. A 'Welcome Meeting' for NQTs is addressed by the County Education Officer and Chief Inspector as a means of demonstrating the importance of NQTs to the LEA. They are given a warm welcome, both physically in the provision of a buffet tea and in the strength of the messages! At this meeting, all of the Inspectors work with small numbers of NQTs, either in secondary specialist groups or primary area groups. This includes an introduction to the work of the Schools' Team and encourages the initial networking of NQTs as a primary objective. Similarly, the team of teacher advisers from the business unit all attend and work in the same groups. The teacher advisers support the rest of the induction programme for the remainder of the school year. This includes a full day conference with a choice of twenty-one seminars, two half-day sessions and a twilight. The programme is differentiated to allow some degree of choice and based upon needs identified by NQTs and induction tutors. The quality of the induction programme is one of the responsibilities of the Inspector for CPD.

The Link Inspector supports the NQT in the first instance by discussing with the headteacher the arrangements for induction. This raises awareness about the implications of statutory induction and ensures that the Career Entry Profile, 10 per cent non-contact time and the need for support, monitoring and assessment are made high-profile issues. In agreeing the use of the Link Inspector's time with the school for the coming term, it may be that a paired observation of the NQT is asked for to support the professional development of the headteacher or induction tutor. This indirectly supports the NQT in ensuring consistency of judgements about the quality of teaching across schools. The Link Inspector may also be involved in observing the NQT teach as part of a monitoring exercise, for example, in evaluating the implementation of the National Numeracy Strategy in a school. In this way NQTs would be given strengths and areas for development to move on their practice in the same way as experienced teachers are seen by inspectors in their Link role.

The specialist Inspector may be called upon if the NQT is experiencing difficulties. Subject or phase specialists will observe practice to give a specialist perspective. One of the responsibilities for the Inspector for CPD is to monitor the assessment process. Following the first assessment report, action is taken if there are NQTs who are failing to make satisfactory progress and who currently are not meeting induction standards. Following liaison with the school and the Link Inspector, teacher adviser support is usually commissioned to work alongside the NQTs. Targets for this support are negotiated to reflect current objectives on the CEP. This LEA intervention is designed to complement school based activities, to ensure that the NQT is effectively supported in a variety of ways and using specific expertise.

In promoting the concept of 'continuing professional development', the content of the summer term's NQT programme is concerned with the building of professional portfolio, with all that this entails in the way of reflection and evaluation. The LEA works with its three beacon schools to extend opportunities for continuing induction to a second year, through the support of beacon funding and the courses they offer. The continuum of PD also works in our links with higher education at the University of Warwick. Valuable contributions are made from the ITT staff in training for induction tutors in exploring the issues relating to 'Standardisation'. The links with the university also support the accreditation of prior learning towards further qualifications at Warwick. This is a partnership between Schools' Team, the University, through the Institute of Education, and the Education Development Service of teacher advisers. Whilst staff in Warwickshire schools can be supported to accredit any prior learning, there is particular emphasis on accrediting the work of induction tutors. In reflecting on the craft of teaching and supporting the development of others, one can become more critically aware of what constitutes effective practice, which in turn leads to further expertise in school improvement.

Promoting school self-evaluation and review

At the heart of school improvement lies the process of systematic and effective self-evaluation. Headteachers, staff and governors need the will, opportunity, skills and tools to examine critically and constructively school performance in its broadest sense. Schools need to be able to monitor and evaluate their essential processes and outcomes; to acknowledge their strengths and successes; and to identify precisely the key areas for improvement and development. A crucial strategic role for the local education authority is to encourage and enable schools to engage confidently and positively in this process.

In recent years Warwickshire inspectors have worked with headteachers, senior managers and subject leaders in using monitoring techniques associated with the OfSTED inspection process. Paired lesson observations and scrutinies of work have provided important professional development opportunities as well as invaluable insights into vital aspects of school performance. However, it was recognised that despite the undoubted benefits of regular externally supported monitoring activities, what schools really needed was a systematic and well-structured process of self-review supplemented by visits from inspectors.

In 1998 Warwickshire inspectors were introduced to the Quality in Education materials developed for schools by Lloyds TSB Group plc from the Business Excellence Model. The 'Excellence Model' provides a well-structured and well-documented process based on nine criteria that are used to assess the competence and success of any organisation (see Figure 6.1). The Excellence Model is based upon the premise that *customer* (parents and pupils) *satisfaction*, *people* (staff) *satisfaction* and a positive *impact on society* are achieved through *leadership* driving *policy and strategy, people management, resources* and *processes*, leading, ultimately, to excellence in *results*. Each one of the criteria is broken down into more specific sub-criteria enabling schools to focus very specifically upon particular issues.

The model is founded upon the principles of Total Quality Management and focuses on continuous improvement. While it was recognised that some of the terminology – 'customer satisfaction' – might be alien to schools, other aspects – 'leadership', 'resources' and 'results' – would be

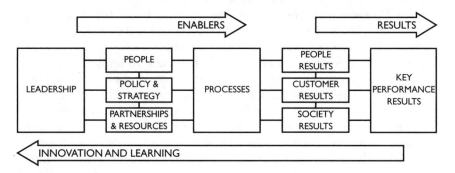

Figure 6.1 The Excellence Model
© EFQM, The EFQM Excellence Model is a registered trademark

familiar. The focus on 'enabler' and 'results' criteria would also encourage schools to look beyond the mere existence of processes and to begin to evaluate more systematically their impact on learners. This seemed prerequisite to successful school improvement.

The Excellence Model has been piloted with a group of headteachers and governors from forty primary, secondary and special schools. The schools included some identified by OfSTED as having serious weaknesses or requiring special measures, for whom the development of systematic approaches to monitoring and evaluation was of paramount importance. Despite some discomfort with elements of the terminology of the Excellence Model, schools were generally enthused by the introductory days, and headteachers and governors expressed a desire to go back to school and try out the tools and strategies.

Three months later the 'pilot schools' were invited back for a 'recall day' to share experiences and comment on the usefulness of the materials. It was particularly satisfying to hear of both the use and the positive impact of a range of approaches. Some schools had made particularly good use of the Excellence Model questionnaires to investigate the perceptions of teachers, non-teaching staff and governors to aspects of the leadership and management of schools. Others had used the model's approach to lesson observations to develop a less threatening, more participative approach to monitoring teaching and learning. The lesson observation schedule involves the teacher in providing structured notes relating to the preparation and proposed delivery of the lesson and also provides the observer with particular issues upon which to focus. The key to the success of the process lies in the requirement for both observer and observed to evaluate the lesson and then share their perceptions before agreeing strategies for improvement. The process has been particularly well received by teachers.

Over the following twelve months up to January 2000 nearly 200 schools have been introduced to the Excellence Model materials. Later this year they will be presented in a revised format which is more school-friendly and which also takes account of the European Foundation for Quality Management's revisions to the Business Excellence Model. The new format will also be available on CD ROM and will contain case study materials drawn from schools across the country.

Apart from introducing schools to the materials an important role for the LEA is to encourage their continued use through disseminating effective practice. The 'recall' days have been useful in enabling schools to present and discuss their experiences. One school has made important amendments to the lesson observation pro forma to better suit the needs of its teachers. Another shared some exciting work undertaken with governors. All agree that the Excellence Model materials are used most effectively where the climate of the school promotes openness and trust. If staff are to be encouraged to be reflective and to evaluate school performance constructively and critically, then they must trust the system and not feel threatened by it. Time spent in ensuring that the climate and ethos are right is time well spent.

While impressed with the Excellence Model we also recognised that OfSTED's School Self-Evaluation training programme provided schools with a review process related directly to the school context. This programme also reflects current political imperatives and ensures that schools undertake self-review against the same criteria that OfSTED inspectors will use. Apart from its use for school improvement, the process is no bad preparation for the very public scrutiny of schools by OfSTED.

The materials offer important opportunities for headteachers, senior managers and subject leaders to practise observing lessons and scrutinising samples of work. The key input from LEA inspectors has been to encourage participants to go beyond description of what they observe into evaluation and judgement.

A further significant role for the LEA has been in updating the OfSTED training programme to take account of revisions to the framework and handbook for inspection. This has enabled schools to acquaint themselves with the current processes and use up-to-date evaluation criteria when making judgements about attainment, progress, teaching, learning and pupils' attitudes and values.

The LEA has thus played a key role in the process of providing schools with a range of skills and strategies for undertaking systematic and structured approaches to self-review. The other key monitoring role is then to ensure that these are being used effectively to support the process of continuing school improvement.

School improvement takes place in schools. Clearly the empathy, expertise and experience of LEA Officers, Inspectors and support staff in encouraging excellence should play a significant role in defining and developing high quality education and promoting high standards, but the dedication and skill of leaders and practitioners in schools, particularly in classrooms, will be the true catalyst and driver of change.

7 Changing roles and functions

Tim Brighouse

One way of looking at the functions, powers and roles of local education authorities is to analyse them over time; to compare as it were their relative importance in different eras of local education authority development. Set out in Table 7.1 is an attempt at assessment on a rising (one – less important to five – more important) scale. The assessment of the relative importance of some general functions and duties and in some specific fields covers three periods – a relatively undisturbed and unchanging first period that lasted from 1944 to 1980; a second period from the passage of the 1988 Act to the election of a Labour Government in 1997; and a third from 1997 to the present day. I have omitted a period of 1980 to 1988 as one of transition, almost a phoney war, as an increasingly confident Conservative Government began to change the rules of engagement with successive pieces of sometimes apparently contradictory legislation which culminated with the 1988 Education Reform Act and a distinctly different climate within which LEAs should operate along more clearly defined market principles.

The assessment set out in Table 7.1 is, of course, personal and to that extent arbitrary and people will disagree with some of the ratings, but it does provide a way of illustrating the changing picture. What the table fails to do of course is to capture a third dimension, namely the way in which central direction has been exercised by the Government over first the curriculum and secondly the way that the curriculum has been taught. What once was a private affair is now the subject of central debate, decision and increasingly detailed direction. It will be to that issue that I return towards the end of this chapter. First, however, let us examine the unfolding story of LEAs which has led to their present position of comparative impotence. For the history of LEAs is one of accelerating decline marked by glimpses of creativity and achievement.

Ronald Arnold's monograph on education development plans for the Education Management Information Exchange (NFER, 1999) is instructive. It shows what 150 local education authorities suspected, namely that the Department for Education and Employment was ensuring you could construct any education development plan you liked so long as it

Table 7.1 An assessment of the changing functions, powers and roles of local
education authorities (1 to 5 on a rising scale of importance)

	1944–1980	1988–1997	1997+
General			
Planning	5	1	5
Providing	5	3	1
Purchasing or securing provision	1	4	5
Promoting education	5	2	5
Managing curriculum	3	1	1
Security equity	2	3	3
Judging equity	4	4	2
Evaluating quality	1	1	5
Specific			
Influence in HE	3	–	–
Influence in FE	4	–	–
Influence in schools	5	2	2
Careers services	5	1	2
Special educational needs	2	5	5
Transport	5	5	5
Early years	1	1	5
School improvement	1	1	4
Youth	5	4	4
Adult	5	5	3

had no more than eight priorities and that literacy, numeracy and improving failing schools were among them. The Ford Motor Car Company in the 1930s would have approved: you can have any car so long as it's black.

Indeed, LEAs have never been more constrained in what they can do than now. A regulatory regime is backed by statute and ensures that the sheer pressure of letters, consultation, advice and inspection from officials in the DfEE, OfSTED and Audit, coupled with a very tight and prescriptive control of LEA spending, have almost extinguished the last vestiges of their creative history.

The Butler 1944 settlement left the Minister – later Secretary of State – with but three powers – the first of authorising the removal of air-raid shelters; the second of controlling the number, supply and distribution of teachers and the third of authorising the opening and closing of school buildings within a rationing system of loans to finance school buildings. So it remained until the 1988 Education Act.

The flavour of the age is encapsulated in the foreword to the Ministry pamphlet 'Story of A School' issued in 1945 and re-issued in the early 1950s.

> The Junior School has escaped much of the limelight which has naturally, in recent years, fallen on secondary education. The importance, however, of reviewing traditional methods and ideas at the junior stage was brought out in the Consultative Committee's Report on the Primary School, issued in 1931, and recently reprinted. Unfortunately, the general principles which should underlie the education of children from seven to eleven, which were so admirably defined in that Report, are still far from being universally practised. The White Paper – 'Educational Reconstruction' – published only five years ago, said: 'Instead of the junior schools performing their proper and highly important function of fostering the potentialities of children at an age when their minds are nimble and receptive, their curiosity strong, their imagination fertile and their spirits high, the curriculum is too often cramped and distorted by over-emphasis on examination subjects and on ways and means of defeating the examiners. The blame for this rests not with the teachers but with the system.'
>
> Improved methods adopted by local education authorities for allocating pupils to secondary schools at the age of eleven are beginning to relieve the examination pressure on the junior schools, and it is hoped that these schools will take full advantage of the new freedom which is being offered to them.
>
> In 'Story of a School' Mr A. L. Stone, formerly headmaster, describes the successful and original work which has been done in the Steward Street Junior School, Birmingham. What he has achieved in an environment which others might well have found discouraging shows how much can be done with courage, sympathy and imagination, and in arranging for the publication of this pamphlet the Minister hopes that it will encourage other teachers to experiment on this and other lines.
>
> The Ministry is indebted to the local education authority for Birmingham for so readily giving permission to publish Mr. Stone's account of his work. Teachers and others will appreciate the authority's desire that the school should not be embarrassed by visitors as a result of the publication of this pamphlet.

Curiously, with one or two exceptions, the LEAs ignored the enormous powers and influence that they had in their hands. Mostly they contented themselves with a quantitative role. That is to say there were new buildings to create. Schools built in the 1950s are distinguished by the generosity of their proportions, lavish in their design and the space of their corridors, cloakrooms, assembly spaces and teaching accommodation. They were designed to be 'fit for the children of returning heroes'.

So LEAs were busy building schools, creating youth service, buying grand old country houses to be adult education centres, working in partnership with the Ministry and teacher training colleges (later to be called the colleges of education, before being transformed into colleges of higher education or parts of universities). Through a system monitored by the 'Pooling Committee', expenditure on 'advanced further education' was used to expand principally the colleges of advanced technology (CATs) which subsequently became the second post-war wave of newer universities after the ones founded in the early 1960s and included in their number places such as Loughborough, Aston and UMIST. But it was also used to create and expand the polytechnics until they too became independent in 1988 and are now recognised as universities and include such names as Sheffield Hallam, Oxford Brookes and the University of Central England.

Merely to recount LEAs' responsibilities and their achievements is to illustrate the immense scope of their power and influence, but it is to describe a world that has gone. The CATs, the polytechnics and all the colleges (including the extensive network of technical or further education colleges) all now enjoy absolute independence and are funded through national systems of one sort of another. The pressures of budgets and the 'capping' of first the rates, then the poll tax and finally the council tax, combined to cause the closure of most of the Outdoor Education Centres and then self-standing Residential Adult Education Centres.

It was not always so. Until the late 1960s, as the birth-rate had expanded, LEAs quantitatively expanded, opening new and expanding existing schools together with other facilities. However, in the 15 to 20 years that followed, as demography went into reverse, the LEAs amalgamated and closed many of the schools and facilities they had so popularly and carefully created. The use of the word 'popular' is apposite; for the reverse process was certainly unpopular. Worse it was messy and badly managed. It was not something envisaged by those who created the system at the end of the war when, at a more generous and optimistic time, it would have been assumed that any downturn in the birth-rate would present a greater chance to improve the quality of what was offered by, for example, improving the pupil/teacher ratio. Nobody had anticipated the oil crisis of the early 1970s, nor the damaging period of student unrest in 1968; still less the simultaneous 'black papers' debate which revealed, where once there was consensus, a growing schism about method and a determination not so much to open the gate to the 'secret garden' of the curriculum as to trample all over it. In short, the second post-war period was marked by falling rolls, shortage of money, union unrest and maladroit LEA management.

It is a period which has its own historians. In a *Generation of Schooling* Harry Judge provides an insight to events from the point of view of a pupil, teacher, headteacher and finally a director of Oxford University's Department of Education. Although the book therefore is written mainly from the vantage point of the classroom and the headteacher's study, Judge was also a member of the James Committee which made extensive recommendations to improve the teaching profession. Through that connection he saw much of the national scene and as founding principal of Banbury School he could provide a glimpse of what it was like to work in one local education authority, Oxfordshire, in the 1960s and 1970s. He was a member too of the influential 'All Souls Group', which meets regularly and has done since the war years, to discuss events and possible directions of the education service.

For what it is worth, Oxfordshire provided an example of that element of LEA practice which was unusual – namely, an overt interest in the quality of what went on in the classroom. Alan Chorlton, the Education Officer at the time, drew his inspiration from other more illustrious contemporaries such as Clegg in the West Riding and Newsom in Hertfordshire. Visits from Chorlton, according to Harry Judge, were events that were memorable since they always ended in a stimulating discussion and a debate about some proposition for educational development. The greatest post-war exponent of such a developmental role in education was Sir Alec Clegg in the West Riding. Indeed, he had been the person first to identify the practice outlined in the leaflet 'Story of a School' during his period as an administrative assistant in Birmingham during the war. The headteacher at that school became his art adviser in the West Riding. It was not that Clegg ignored the administrative and managerial imperatives of his job, for there was no LEA more active in quantitative activity with generous expansion of new embellishments to the LEA system whether in the fields of outdoor education, the youth service, adult education, further or teacher education provision. It was Clegg however who expanded what might rather grandly be called the pedagogical role of the LEA. Of course he was interested in ensuring that there should be more education, but he was also vitally interested in both the 'how' and the 'why' of education. His reputation for being interested in teaching and learning and what went on in the classroom was so great that even now, thirty years after he retired, teachers who retire in other parts of the country far from the West Riding, but who had contact and experience of the West Riding in their early career, see fit to comment on it. Dozens of times in the last five years I have heard the words 'I met Alec Clegg only once, but . . .' to be followed by a wistful encomium about a golden age when people at all levels of the system were interested in the process of teaching and learning and the value of the quality of the practitioner. That may have been true of the West Riding, but it was not in most other parts of the LEA system. There were others like Sylvester in Bristol, Wilson in Shropshire, Mason in Leicestershire, Morris in Cambridgeshire and Newsom in Hertfordshire, who drew attention to their schools' practices and thereby their authorities as places where there was support for experimentation, innovation and the intellectual curiosity which produces debate and educational advance. But they were rare. Moreover, most people who looked at their practice identified only the systemic innovations – the service manifestations as it were – rather than the substance of something to copy. So the Leicestershire system of junior high schools with a break at 14, Henry Morris's 'village colleges' and Alec Clegg's 'middle schools' were copied rather than this attention to, and interest in, what went on in the classroom.

So Judge's illustration in 'A Generation of Schooling' of Oxfordshire practice is of a rare education authority where Chorlton in a quieter way went about emulating these other great contemporaries. So he recruited his primary officer, Edith Moorhouse, from the West Riding and she worked with a maverick HMI and distinguished etcher, Robin Tanner, in proceeding to transform primary practice so it was possible to see the distinctive features of what made an Oxfordshire primary school in almost all its schools. This was brought into sharp relief for me, because on local government reorganisation in 1974 Oxfordshire took over the very different and disparate primary practice in primary schools formerly controlled by Oxford City and Berkshire. It is true to say that the influence of LEAs in that period was so great that I could be blindfolded and driven to a particular school and then asked to describe whether I was in an old Berkshire school, an old Oxford City school, or an old Oxfordshire school.

As has been indicated this world changed in 1988. The earlier disappearance of the West Riding before the period of falling rolls and contraction had merely served to highlight the contrast between the world that it had been and the golden era when compared with a more lilliputian present occupied by LEAs which had cut budgets, closed schools, made teachers and other staff redundant and joined in the debate, which by then was gathering pace, of a decline in standards.

The 1988 Act gave the Secretary of State over 300 powers where previously he had three. There was to be a National Curriculum with a multitude of specific 'attainment targets', a battery of tests at 7, 11 and 14 to supplement GCSE at age 16. Detailed control of schools' spending by tightly focused local rules about the proportion to be spent separately on teachers, support staff, books, equipment, telephones and the like was to be totally replaced by the introduction, either immediately or over three years, of 'local management of schools' whereby a pupil-led formula in the main gave schools the bulk of their expenditure to use as they saw fit. (It is perhaps worth commenting on a very small development in that period which foreshadowed the paradoxical gathering central control, namely the introduction by Sir Keith Joseph of half a percentage point of the total education budget to be spent on what were called education support grants. These were used initially to promote a revolution in the teaching of basic English and maths in the mid-1980s.)

LEAs were encouraged by the Audit Commission post-1988 to focus on two issues; first: the colleges of further education and their strategic management and funding; and secondly, the question of the monitoring and inspection of schools. Legislation less than four years later however removed both functions from LEAs, who were left mainly as the hand-maidens of a centrally directed DfEE. Most LEAs retreated either into per-petuating, as far as they could, habits of behaviour towards schools that were scarcely appropriate in a pre-education reform era, or into being reactive and into providing whatever the schools wanted them to do, keeping alive the spirit of being interested in the quality of what went on in the classroom moreover. A few LEAs decided on a different route.

These authorities could see that for all its frenetic activities the DfEE was missing the point which people like Clegg had focused on – namely, the quality of teaching and learning. So one or two authorities decided to concentrate their efforts on 'school improvement'. The work of researchers into 'school effectiveness' since the late 1970s had afforded much sharper insight into a knowledge of those characteristics of school organisation and practice which seemed to be associated with more successful schools. The 'school improvement' researchers had begun to work on this and identify those processes which on an everyday basis were exercising the practice of schooling and vitally *how* they were exercised with a greater or lesser likelihood of reducing the characteristics identified by the researchers into 'school effectiveness'. The belief of the 'school improvers' group of LEAs was that if you could equip schools with a 'shared language' to look at each other's whole school practice you could enable them to learn more quickly from each other's practice and from research. Hammersmith and Fulham LEA would be the authority which others would identify as an authority most thorough in its determination to equip its schools' communities with knowledge of school improvement techniques. Perhaps it is not coincidence that the Director of Education of that particular LEA had immediately previously been a headteacher.

In Birmingham also the LEA attempted to harness within a school improvement agenda some very specific interventions. So the city pro-moted target setting for higher standards of literacy and numeracy within a system of guarantees. There were three separate guarantees for the early years, primary and secondary schooling respectively. Each had targets of input guaranteeing a secure funding base for schools, targets of experience outlining certain essential activities that any pupil could expect to encounter during the course of their career and targets for outcome represented in ever higher standards in, for example, literacy and numer-acy at aged 11 and GCSE at 16. Significantly these targets were generated from the bottom-up rather than the top-down. The theory was that for target setting to be effective it had to start with the learners sharing a map of learning and the understanding of the journey of progressive under-standing and skill acquisition with which they were engaging. It is a process which fits well with 'formative assessment' first fully and widely outlined in the TGAT Report (Task Group on Assessment and Testing) chaired by Professor Paul Black and undertaken to create an assessment framework for the newly designed National Curriculum in 1989. 'Formative assessment', however, has since been somewhat neglected as the 'summative', 'informative' and 'comparative' practices of assessment have been emphasised by the publication of league tables, OFSTED's PANDA analysis and presently performance related pay.

The successful teacher then uses her own knowledge of how the learner might proceed to master the skill or understanding of the concept to engage the learner in activity designed to do precisely that. Knowing a great deal about the obstacles different learners had previously encountered in the process, and drawing on her knowledge of the particular learner involved, as well as the use of different resources and teaching and learning aids, the teacher thus helps the learner to achieve the learning 'target'. A vital ingredient in that process is the learner's own knowledge of the progress he or she thinks he/she is making towards the goal – in other words, self-assessment against a map of criteria to which the teacher responds. This process is at the heart of 'formative assessment'. Sometimes the teacher involves others or arranges learners in particular groupings or sets in order to sweeten the process of learning. But the most effective teacher shares with the learner the purpose of her changes in organisation.

Any successful teacher of, say, a group of 8-year-olds will know what they have achieved with previous groups and will take delight both in demonstrating the ways in which any subsequent group can out-perform what previous groups have achieved either in scope or in the reach of their learning journey. 'I never had as good a Year 4 as this one' the teacher will confide to colleagues. Equally on occasion the group will not be as well prepared by a colleague as in earlier years, or will have encountered circumstances beyond the school that put the achievement of a year-on-year comparison of standards at risk. For example, there may suddenly be an influx of asylum seekers. For the thoughtful, experienced and skilled teacher that represents an 'all in a professional day's work' challenge to which they patiently respond.

Discussions like these dominated the discourse about target setting within Birmingham in the mid-1990s as schools were invited to consider setting 'ever higher targets' – in short, as we put it, to 'improve on previous best' – and perhaps measure themselves on a three-year rolling average as we wrestled to change a culture of 'what more can you expect from children from backgrounds like this' to one where the sky is the limit so far as ever higher standards of achievement are concerned. The 'improving on previous best' became our strap-line as we sought to identify those targeted interventions which seemed to hold out the most promise of success as the LEA at the centre tried to change the climate locally to one which would be supportive of the teachers' efforts to raise standards. Amongst these were the creation of a Children's University and a University of the First Age to provide a mix of holiday learning, after school learning experiences and supported self-study opportunities; a climate calendar establishing successive years of Reading, Number, the Arts, Science etc. and a major quality development and professional development programme. We also collected and published what were called 'butterflies', or tiny interventions which, given the right climate, or adjusted to suit different circumstances, appeared to offer disproportionate chances of success. One example serves to make the point.

Annual learning plans

Description

The staff of this school, including teachers, learning assistants, integration assistants and non-teaching staff wanted to show their commitment to learning and personal development in their ambition to create a true, learning school. Governors were also encouraged to participate. Accordingly they agreed to fill out on an annual basis a single pro forma which set out their learning targets in terms of acquiring knowledge and understanding, developing skills, work shadowing and general professional development.

Processes involved

- Teaching and learning
- Creating an environment
- Collective review
- Staff development

Comment on impact

The staff felt appropriately challenged to set themselves personal learning targets and were pleased to share with each other their rate of progress. In some cases they relied on each other to develop certain skills (for example, those related to information technology) or acquire particular knowledge. When the learning plans were reviewed by a person of their choice they were delighted at their success. Some have now formalised their learning plans into obtaining further qualifications. Altogether the school can justly say that with its pupils, parents and governors, it is a learning community.

Some of these practices seemed so obvious we encouraged their adoption across the city, not by imposition but by judicious prompting. Schools created their own books of butterflies. As we focused on schools which appeared to be successful we found more practice which needed to be catalogued and discussed in order that other schools had a good chance of improving their practice.

We were able to embark on this strategy by virtue of three factors specific to school improvement. First we established a common language of the principles, processes and purposes of school improvement. The seven processes were identified as:

- The practice of teaching and learning
- The exercise of leadership
- The practice of management and organisation
- The practice of collective review
- The creation of an environment most suitable for learning
- The promotion of staff development
- The encouragement of parental and community involvement.

Our purpose in describing these processes was to construct a map, so that schools might have a better chance of understanding:

- How to achieve the characteristics
- The practice of schools in similar or dissimilar circumstances – benchmarking
- The findings of researchers

Second, we had a rich database which was very well analysed by a small unit led by a statistician whose interest in teaching and learning was palpable. All schools were provided with annual, statistical profiles which could be analysed in dozens of different ways so that for example statistically reliable groups or families of primary schools could be encouraged to compare their performance and learn from each other. Standards could also be monitored over time analysing achievement by race, gender and special education needs. Thirdly, the Advisory Service more or less sang from the same song-sheet and became sufficiently familiar with the main themes that good practice could be noted and spread. Most importantly of all, the balance of support over pressure was continually reinforced not simply by public experiments, but by thousands of private and personal commendations which reinforced the practitioner and the support service.

Birmingham's pioneering work on target setting, however, was soon swamped by DfEE's adoption of it following the election of a new Labour Government in 1997. Once the 'bottom-up' nature of the target setting was replaced by 'top-down', imposed expectations of what could or could not be achieved, linked to a 'naming and shaming' approach meant there was an emphasis on pressure and sticks rather than the support and carrot. The agenda which had been created in the ownership of a few local education authorities was wrested from them and applied across the whole country.

It was as though, just as the colleges, the polytechnics and the curriculum were variously nationalised, or given their independence, so the very 'ideas themselves' were made into an orthodoxy from which no-one should depart.

It had reminded me of nothing so much as the time in the mid-1980s when a smaller group of pioneering authorities, principally Oxfordshire, Somerset, Leicestershire and Coventry in one consortium; the ILEA in London; Essex and some others in third consortium and some northern authorities in a fourth, all pioneered in their different ways what came to be known as the National Record of Achievement. But by the time it was so named it had been ruined by the dead hand of national imposition. What had started in a Wiltshire secondary school under a teacher called Don Stansbury fifteen years earlier (before it had been transported tenderly to a school in Totnes, Devon) had then been gently cultivated among sets of teachers in pioneering authorities. These teachers were given time to debate and redefine what should be included in the certificate so that there could be, and was, a sensitive understanding at school level of the implications for teaching and learning practice of the adoption of the scheme. The sudden national adoption of the scheme across 5,000 secondary schools did not allow such processes of local staff development to continue at a pace chosen by the school as appropriate for it. It seems impossible to have *optional* schemes at a national level.

Most dangerously in recent times there is a certainty about ideas themselves nationally, which seems at variance with not merely research findings but the lessons of educational history.

In 1998 the Audit Commission set out its view of the future of LEAs in their publication 'Held in Trust'. From that one might conclude that the Birmingham model setting out a broad strategic vision and supplementing it with a clearly thought through focus on school improvement, with a few priorities all backed by cognitive action plans is the right one. But as the earlier part of this chapter pointed out, the evidence from the education development plans, let alone the myriad of other plans, is that they are all remarkably similar and that if they are not, they do not get approved. Moreover, the OfSTED/Audit framework for learning and inspection now leaves very little room for manoeuvre about how the plans should be carried through and the functions of an LEA discharged. Yet once again the nature of the Educational Development Plan imposed by DfEE is worlds away from the Strategic Plan which Birmingham, for example, had pioneered.

So what role remains for LEAs, apparently tied to an increasingly specific national agenda? Let us examine the possible roles.

It seems doubtful that the role of harnessing a database in order to match schools in comparable circumstances can be discharged more effectively locally than it can be nationally. After all, save for the very largest authority, there is unlikely to be a sufficiently large sample of schools in comparable circumstances to match one school with another in order to compare notes and learn from each other. On the other hand, as

Figure 7.1 shows, it is possible for an LEA sufficiently large like Birmingham to pioneer what will one day become a national phenomenon, that of comparing the relative improvement rates at schools against absolute levels of performance. Figure 7.1 provides an example of such comparison at Key Stage 2 in Birmingham's junior schools. But something similar can and is done for secondary schools. Figure 7.2 illustrates the same junior schools measured for added value when eligibility for free school meals is taken into account. There is no doubt, however, that one of the next steps in school improvement is to use such data and similar data much more precisely at school level. LEAs will need to pioneer that, in order that any national scheme is less crudely founded than it might otherwise be.

One of the elusive issues in school improvement is how to establish an achievement culture in circumstances – normally urban and challenging – where the achievement culture does not exist beyond the school gates. *Access and Achievement in Urban Areas* (OfSTED, 1993) illustrated that schools very rarely have within themselves the capacity to improve in a sustainable way. While *Improving City Schools* (OfSTED, 2000) points out the phenomenon and helpfully focuses on the 'in-school' factors, which in combination can improve such schools, it is silent on the 'beyond school' issue.

Here surely is an issue for the role of some LEAs in school improvement. There are what may be called 'vulnerable schools' in many LEAs where the environmental context – usually desolate urban landscapes with

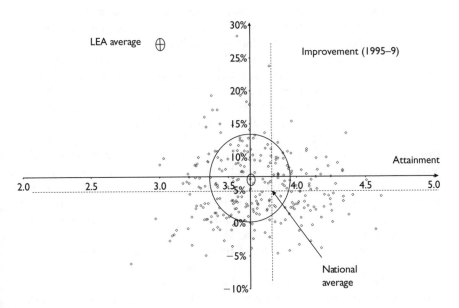

Figure 7.1 End of Key Stage 2 National Curriculum assessments: 1995–9 (rolling average point score) school compared to LEA average

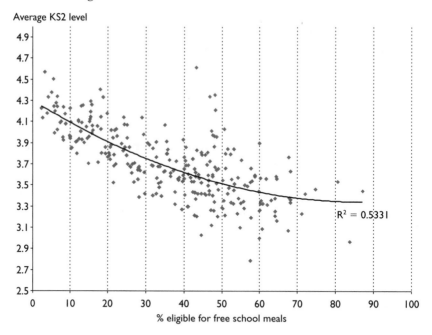

Figure 7.2 School by school comparison of average Key Stage 2 level (1997–9) with proportion of pupils eligible for free school meals

high unemployment, poverty, violence, drugs, crime and domestic inability – so stack the odds against successful educational outcomes in schools, especially in the teenage years, that some collective intervention locally is essential. In such areas all the research suggests that schools on their own cannot reliably succeed. Agendas relating to health, to housing, to social services, to police and other agencies impinge seriously on the school's capacity to succeed against the odds. The only body with a remit to straddle those agendas is the local democratic authority. Indeed, the recent Local Government Act (2000) provides authorities with new powers to exercise such as a general co-ordinating role and function of promoting the 'economic, social and environmental well being of their community' and 'the duty to prepare and maintain a community strategy'. Moreover, the role of securing and maintaining 'partnerships' across these various agencies to support school improvement and the broader duty in an increasingly fragmented world lies with the local authority.

Of course it could be argued that this does not mean that local authorities in mapping and maintaining 'partnerships' have to have a role in affecting the provision itself. But it does mean that they have the responsibility for judging what is necessary and for brokering such support. Moreover, in the case of 'vulnerable schools' there is often an unpredictable urgency in intervention where a sudden combination of events renders a school, hitherto successful, or reasonably successful, at immediate and serious risk. For example, the departure of some key staff, the illness of a senior manager, a failure to recruit staff, a change in a governing body leading to a confusion of role – all can and do destabilise vulnerable schools in challenging circumstances. In Birmingham, to cite but one case, we could observe one local school – a GM school controlled by the Funding Agency for Schools – which was in special measures and in a state of continued and accelerated decline. In the end it was the LEA not the FAS which had to supply a headteacher and new governors for the school and to seek to start – as it happened successfully, although very belatedly – the long process of renewal and recovery. In a heavily urban area it is diffi-cult to secure sufficient high-quality governors to feel confident in the success of schools which are so autonomous that they would have only one further democratic check in their governance beyond the level of school and nothing at Central Government. (Of course this is not to rule out regional government and influence.)

What it rules in unambiguously, however, is that there needs to be, beyond the school, room for educational vision and leadership which is, or could be, subtly different from the national perspective and tailored to local circumstance. There is in any case no certain answer or orthodoxy in education. Successful learning is more to do with questions, with experi-ment and with building on provisional theory. Above all, it is an activity which depends on building relationships from the bottom. Any regional or local administration divorced from local democracy would fail that test and might be affected by the secrecy and closed nature of Central Govern-ment which demands of all its civil servants that they sign a declaration under the Official Secrets Act. Clearly senior civil servants are not averse to bringing that to their aid whenever it becomes embarrassing that an heretical view of colleagues might be 'leaked' to the press. It is hard to imagine that there are school matters that should be subject to such undue secrecy.

The problem remains one exposed by OfSTED/Audit Reports, namely that in places where there are lots of vulnerable schools the LEA may be so small that it cannot either recruit the calibre of staff, or mount sufficient 'fire-power' (i.e. be sufficiently large that it can harness competent resources) to help vulnerable schools out of their difficulties.

While it may be seductive to think that the answer is to create a private market of providers sufficiently large that they could meet the needs of all schools, such a solution fails to take account of two factors. First, such private providers will not necessarily identify the sudden shifts in perform-ance – often brought to light by the democratic voice – because they will be performing to a contract out with the local authority. And the second objection is that they will fail to take account of the vital role of the elected councillor in relation to the governing body mentioned earlier. The facts are that in urban areas the governing body itself is frequently the source of the dysfunctionality and where the role of the city councillor then becomes a vital part of the solution.

All this is arguing therefore in heavily urbanised areas for a large democratically controlled education authority with a clear and wide role in school improvement.

The last issue for challenge is that of urging authorities slavishly to follow the principle of 'intervening in inverse proportion to success'. Of course it is a sensible general principle, but unimaginative adherence to it, which is encouraged by OfSTED/Audit, could lead to difficulties.

Consider one example, namely the accelerating use of the technologies for learning. In this field nobody at present is confident of being able to identify, analyse and spread the burgeoning examples of good practice. Yet such practice has profound implications for the running of schools whether in the call on supply teachers, or in promoting early accredited success for pupils (while not seeing that as a timetabling problem) or in the motivation of pupils and classroom organisation and practice. To intervene in 'inverse proportion to success' however is to miss seeing the leading edge of this new learning: it is to be perpetually, ever so slightly, behind the pace. An obvious illustration may be drawn from the field of innovation in ICT, but it is also true in school improvement and teaching and learning generally, even if not on such a dramatic scale.

In short, if we have moved from a 'dependent' to an 'independent' model of schooling, but if the social inclusion agenda calls for 'interdependence', we need more than an LEA of last resort to promote it.

Moreover, I remain convinced that it is the interest in teaching and learning that is the vital ingredient in leadership exercised at a local level. The reasons are many and all to do with stakeholders.

First, the main local activity is learning and teaching, or support for the learning process. If one measures outcomes as indicators of its success it would be bound to include test and exam results; successful participation and completion rates post-16; progress made by children with special educational needs in overcoming the obstacles to their learning; participation and successful achievement in the arts and sport and in young citizenship activities of one sort or another. One could add a range of other indicators associated with lifelong learning. All that needs to be debated, reflected upon, assessed comparatively and celebrated. Unless a lot of the time of the leadership of the service locally is taken up with that, the individual school misses out on the chance to be affected by, and in their turn influence more effectively, the whole local climate of support for learning. That has never been more important than now as we move away from an age which offered reasonably well-paid employment to large numbers of people who were unskilled and semi-skilled – in short, where failure in academic and other achievement at school was not necessarily a barrier to a job which at least promised the continuing dignity of a wage. Now it is crucial to an individual's long-term financial security, as well as their peace of mind, that levels of education and training are raised substantially.

So we can see that the capacity of the local leader to talk persuasively about teaching and learning is now ever so gently moving into other more economic areas. Indeed, each school's efforts in helping the most challenged and despairing families to come to terms with that shift of lead and expectation demands some co-ordination at a local level of those services. Somebody locally needs to be able to speak cogently about the inter-connections and they need to do it from the viewpoint of the educator. Partnerships do not happen, they need to be created and sustained – even sometimes discontinued when they no longer serve their intended purpose.

So education officers who do not know and understand something about the realities of the classroom on a daily basis will not convince practitioners. But equally, if they do not easily follow the inter-play of policies of the different agencies, whether Education, Social Services, Sport, Housing or Health, they are unlikely to be able both to paint a coherent picture either to the elected member responsible for the overall scene, or to practitioners who are on a daily basis dealing with the family and individual crisis and breakdown on the one hand and on the other providing a purposeful and focused set of learning experiences, both for the individual in distress and the rest of their learning group. Outside a democratic local framework such administrators or local leaders seem unlikely to be able to do that. There is little evidence of it in the Civil Service and the Government Offices themselves confirm the very independent and sometimes insular line which Service Departments of State, such as Health, Education and Social Services, often take.

The major contribution therefore of a local education authority is to be perpetually at the leading edge of practice, challenging Central Government, seeing much more clearly as though with a microscope the real conditions of schooling and being answerable to the local community who see the organisation of schooling as the cradle of democracy itself.

Interlude

Vanessa Wiseman
Headteacher, Langdon School, Newham LEA

Langdon is an 11–16 school of over 1,900 students. It is inclusive, multicultural and co-educational. In 1998 it became a sports college and from September 2000 a beacon school.

Too often in my view, schools' partnerships with LEAs are seen as one end or the other of a continuum. At one end would be a school that really would prefer to be totally independent and is waiting to be unshackled and fly or at the other a school that relies on the LEA for total support and part of a dependency culture. In reality most schools are at different points along the continuum at different times and depending on their context. At Langdon we have developed a relationship with our local LEA, Newham, which is not at either end of the continuum but is rather marked by a mixture of independence, sharing of ideas and practice and partnership. Having joined Newham in 1992, as headteacher of Langdon, I came within a month of the appointment of the current Director of Education, to an LEA that had taken a thorough and reflective look at itself and decided it needed to work hard on raising standards of achievement across the LEA and was committed to doing so. Headteachers and school staff in the LEA have been very active players in this process and have worked with LEA staff to develop a range of initiatives focused on raising of achievement.

At Langdon our work with the LEA can be characterised in three ways. First, we have worked closely and openly with the LEA in developing a central service that meets our needs. We have supported retention of central services, but at the same time have been open about improvements in quality we believed were needed. This has also meant that where colleagues from central services have worked with the school, e.g. in support of inclusive practice, we have needed to ensure that they had a good quality of support and involvement by our school staff. Largely we feel we have been heard and good responsive relationships have developed and consequently supported the achievement of our students.

Second, there are areas where, as a large and innovative organisation, we have a range of external networks and partnerships that we have developed, to support the school's achievements. These range from professional development providers to providers of site services, such as design and decoration. These providers meet a need that the LEA, within its resources, cannot give and also give a healthy breadth to the range of advice, ideas and creativity we can draw on, widening out our experience to further good and creative practice.

Third, we believe our partnership with the LEA should be interactive. There are areas in which we have developed good practice through involvement in a range of wider national initiatives and from our experience we feed back our ideas into the LEA and contribute to the leadership of new developments in, e.g., sports, study support, leadership and management and self-evaluation. It has been important for the LEA to recognise that they cannot always be the leaders on school improvement but must encourage shared leadership with schools and build on the strengths that individual schools can share with others.

Our work on raising achievement exemplifies the balance identified earlier. We have benefited from a range of external partnerships with Langdon including higher education, e.g. on primary transition with the Institute of Education, joint projects such as that developed by the DfEE and Strathclyde University on self-evaluation and our long term work with an educational consultant on team and whole school leadership and currently the Excellence Model. Alongside this we have worked closely with the LEA to further raise achievement. On occasions this has been through the Curriculum Support and Advisory Team, who have worked with specific departments to develop and strengthen practice, worked with new Heads of Department and lead INSET. This work has been successful as a result of a cleat focus and jointly agreed outcomes and is tailored to the needs of the school. In return we contribute to INSET, sharing the developed practice with other schools and colleagues.

A particularly positive development has been the work with the Schools Monitoring and Standards Officer, who originally was the link inspector for the school but has changed and honed his role to meet changing needs of school, LEA and national context. He has been, throughout his work with the school, a critical friend who has helped sharpen our focus by working with team leaders and with the senior team management. He asks the probing questions, helps interpret data and is able to either contribute to improving practice or can help us to access further advice if we need it. Annually he will be part of the school achievement review process in which we put our achievements over the last year into context and develop our targets for the coming year and present and discuss these with governors. It is a role that is both supportive and demanding but importantly is carried out with a knowledge of the school's intake and context. As headteacher, it provides me with intellectual challenge and ensures accountability. The long-termness of the relationship also means it has a developmental quality that allows year on year improvement rather than a series of snapshot visits. It also ensures that the LEA have an informed picture of what good practice is taking place in the school that would be worth sharing with others. Whilst a positive relationship, the edge of targets to meet and challenges of new developments never allows it to be cosy!

In short, the work with the LEA has been a positive strength in our development marked as it is by open dialogue based on frank and often challenging exchange of views, a recognition we are equal partners and a wish to share and build on each partner's strengths.

8 School improvement partnerships

Aiming high, including all – a framework for partnerships to improve urban schooling

Mark Pattison and Steve Munby

In this chapter we outline a suggested framework for analysing and under-standing the challenges which schools and LEAs face at the beginning of the twenty-first century, particularly in urban areas. This framework is then used to examine some of the strategies which LEAs and schools can use to respond to these challenges.

The framework has been developed from our experiences in Blackburn with Darwen. In some respects this is a case study of a small, urban northern LEA in the late 1990s, but it is one we believe may have some relevance and use for others.

Blackburn with Darwen became a new unitary LEA on 1 April 1998. The new Council faced major challenges – from the time when we began to work with the 84 schools in Blackburn with Darwen through the first twelve months of the LEA, nine schools were in special measures, another six had serious weaknesses, and a further eight were a cause for concern. School improvement was thus the number one priority, although set within an overall commitment to lifelong learning and the regeneration of communities.

We bid for and secured one of the first Education Action Zones in the country. For us zones provided an opportunity for collaboration between schools, new resources with few strings attached, creative and innovative approaches and new partnerships. We were determined that the EAZ and the LEA would work together for school improvement and community regeneration and add value to each other.

In 1999 we were awarded beacon status for education under the theme of 'tackling school failure' (not a title we would have chosen). We now have one school in special measures and two with serious weak-nesses and we still have much to learn. However, we can claim to have made a difference. The processes we have been through have been learn-ing experiences for us and we hope they may be instructive and useful to others.

A possible framework for the challenges of urban schooling

As we worked with schools the complexity of the issues and the challenges faced by schools, particularly in deprived urban areas became clear. This is not to say that schools in rural or more affluent areas do not have challenges. However, the interplay of factors in many urban areas undoubtedly intensifies those challenges. This includes features of multiple deprivation such as low income, high unemployment and poor housing, health and education. In addition the intensity, scale and concentration of these factors combine with the dynamic change and diversity of urban life to provide a potent mix.

A framework began to emerge which helped us to begin to make sense of the challenges and therefore how to respond. This is not an academic framework and may not be entirely robust, but it seems to reflect the reality we found on the ground in Blackburn with Darwen and our experiences in other urban areas. The danger of this kind of model is that it stereotypes, exaggerates and oversimplifies. The hope is that whilst recognising that the reality is more complex and each situation unique, this framework can be used as a tool for analysing challenges and considering the possible responses. The framework is outlined in Figure 8.1 and consists of four separate but interlocking dimensions.

THE CHALLENGES

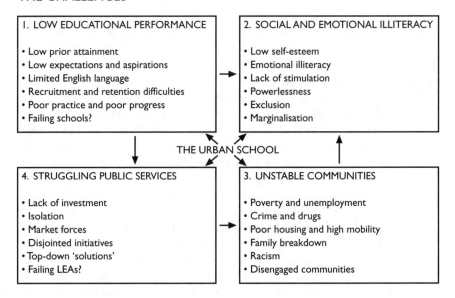

Figure 8.1 The challenges of urban schooling

Low educational performance

This is the most obvious and immediately relevant aspect. Many children enter urban schools with *low prior attainment* and from homes where formal educational achievement has been limited. In such circumstances *low expectations and aspirations* predominate. It is rarely the case that parents do not care about their children's education – often they care passionately – but they don't expect to succeed nor do they know how to access the best from the system and they easily come to accept low performance.

Many children have a *restricted use of the English language*. This is most obvious among ethnic minority pupils for whom English is not the home language. However, language limitations are not confined to ethnic minority children. Many poor white children enter schools with limited language skills and find accessing the curriculum a challenge.

For schools in these areas there is an accumulation of problems. They may have *difficulty in recruiting and retaining teachers*. Those they recruit are often highly committed at first but reach burn-out quickly or become disillusioned and cynical. Even for those schools where children make reasonable progress the published SATs or GCSE scores compare unfavourably with other schools. This has a negative impact on the image of the school in the community and depresses expectations further.

Perhaps it is not so surprising after working in that kind of environment for some time, that some teachers, headteachers and governors also expect little. Our experience is that the phrase 'what can you expect from children brought up in this way' is alarmingly common. In reality the evidence which teachers often see gives them little reason to believe that these children can succeed. A fatalistic attitude has descended on some schools – it isn't that they don't want to succeed, it is that they don't really believe they can make a difference – they are struggling against the tide and feel it almost inevitable that the waves will overwhelm them in the end.

There is poor practice in some urban schools. There are still headteachers who are working extremely hard but not necessarily on the most important things and who choose to avoid the difficult issues, even though they know that they won't go away. There are deputies and curriculum co-ordinators who haven't properly embraced their role and who hark back to the days when being the deputy or the English co-ordinator meant a very different thing to what it means now. There are teachers who settle for second best and collude with underachievement. They are satisfied with a word when they should expect a sentence, satisfied with a sentence when they should expect a paragraph, satisfied with simple vocabulary when they should expect technical vocabulary and they are satisfied with order when they should expect good behaviour and learning. When you walk into some urban schools there is a feeling of being embattled, ground-down, defeated.

There are a far higher proportion of special measures schools in urban areas with high deprivation than nationally. This is probably not a true reflection of the position, as there is little doubt that it is harder to come out of OfSTED well in deprived and challenging areas. The fact remains, however, that far too many schools in urban areas are struggling to provide an adequate education.

There are, of course, many exceptions: individual teachers, head-teachers and whole schools that demonstrate higher levels of achievement. In many schools there is a positive, can-do approach throughout the staff and throughout the school. There is humour, pace, good relationships, challenge, focus, energy and fun. As one successful headteacher in Blackburn with Darwen who has helped to lead her school out of Special Measures said: 'Successful teachers are happy teachers – they look forward to tomorrow.' Some schools triumph in spite of their adverse situation.

Social and emotional illiteracy

It is important to stress that many children and young people from urban areas are well adjusted, come from good supportive homes and arrive at school ready to learn. However, it is equally true that many do not. The numbers of children experiencing some combination of family break up, domestic violence, abuse and drug dependency was almost certainly increasing through the 1980s and 1990s. Even where these are not present, inadequate parenting in conditions of poverty are common – although all of us with children of our own know to be careful not to underestimate how challenging parenting is for us all. The result is many children in our schools who are emotionally disturbed, with *low self-esteem* and have difficulty in forming positive relationships. They are neither ready to learn nor able to behave appropriately. As one headteacher in Blackburn with Darwen said, 'they are not really bad kids, they just lack the social skills and are very challenging because they actually don't know how to behave or even what counts as acceptable behaviour'.

Daniel Goleman has characterised this as *emotional illiteracy*. His review of the research shows 'a worldwide trend for the present generation of children to be more troubled emotionally than the last: more lonely and depressed, more angry and unruly, more nervous and prone to worry, more impulsive and aggressive' (Goleman, 1996: xiii). Goleman argues that deficits in emotional and social competencies are frequently directly related to poor educational performance. A child's readiness to learn is related to their abilities to understand, express and control their emotions. Our recent understanding of the functioning of the brain suggest that if a child is emotionally disturbed then their ability to learn is neurologically impaired. Schools in urban areas are more often dealing with more children who are socially and emotionally illiterate.

A related area is the *lack of stimulation* and the limited range of experiences associated with many of these children, particularly in their early years. Learning is, at least in part, about reflections on and responses to new and stimulating experiences. For some children their early lives lack such stimulation and as a result they have yet to learn how to learn.

Worse still some children and families see no point in learning and cannot or will not engage with the learning process. There is a fatalism and belief it is 'not for them'. This is partly about a feeling of *powerlessness*. They see schools as alien institutions, so different from the home and community. They feel they have no stake in them and have neither the skills or knowledge, nor the confidence to access services. They also find the curriculum largely irrelevant to their experiences.

The result of all the above is a number children that are a challenge to teach. Some schools have responded by either formally *excluding* those *pupils* in large numbers or by adopting policies and practices which effectively exclude them from the mainstream of the school. And let us be clear, it *is* tough for teachers to manage in these situations. It is often the accumulation of such children which is the challenge – one or two such pupils in a class is manageable but when it reaches a critical mass it can become very hard. Add to this parental perceptions that a disruptive minority are adversely affecting the education of the majority and the pressures on schools are considerable.

Unstable communities

A number of factors characterise communities in the industrial north of England but also elsewhere. *Poverty and unemployment* have the most profound effect not only on the material circumstances that children experience but also their readiness for learning. It is not uncommon in urban areas for children to arrive in school ill-nourished, badly clothed and unhealthy. There is a strong link between poor health and low educational achievement.

Crime and drugs frequently go hand-in hand. In lives that are otherwise boring and limited the excitement and stimulation of drugs or juvenile disorder is tempting. This spills over into schools in a variety of ways. One headteacher tells of three children from the same family who arrived in school late one morning with a scrap of paper tightly gripped in one hand. It was to tell the headteacher there had been a raid on the house in the middle of the night. A number of police had burst in making as much noise as possible, searching every room with dogs and taken away the mother and stepfather, leaving the children with the community policewoman. The impact of that experience on those children was profound. The impact on the community of drugs is far reaching including violence, theft and family feuding.

Poor housing and high mobility. Much has been written about Britain's 'run-down estates' and the image is often of failed council housing. But in Blackburn and elsewhere it is also private housing which has been in a state of disrepair. The impact on schools and pupils is very real. Whilst the Government talks of the importance of homework, many children not only have no room with the peace and quiet to study but not even a table in the house on which to work. A related problem is the high mobility rates as families move from one community to another and from one part of the country to another. In some urban schools less than 30 per cent of children that start in a primary school are still there at the end.

The increase in *family breakdown* is high everywhere but poverty makes it worse. In many schools the two-parent family is the exception and the circumstances often leave children feeling uncertain, fearful, guilty and sad.

Racism is not confined to urban areas but poverty and unemployment probably exacerbate it. Physical and verbal abuse of individuals, families and whole communities remains common. More subtle forms of racism are evident in the operation of a number of institutions in the public and private sectors, including schools. Many ethnic minority communities feel undervalued, discriminated against and under threat. There are also frequent tensions between minority communities. All this spills over into schools. Ethnic diversity can be a real strength to a school but it would be foolish to ignore the challenges it poses.

The result (or is it the cause) of all this can be *disengaged communities*. People who feel they are not in the mainstream of society and find it hard to relate to the institutions and aspirations represented by the education system.

Struggling public services

Despite the fact that the twentieth century saw a huge growth in public services they often remain inadequate for or overwhelmed by the task. They have faced an uncertain future from both Conservative and Labour Governments.

Some of that is sheer *lack of investment*. The physical state of school buildings is often poor. In one northern LEA until very recently 30 per cent of schools had roofs that leaked so badly they had to take at least one classroom out of action every time it rained. In Blackburn with Darwen, when we were discussing a PFI project, the funding for maintenance assumed by the private sector for one school was more than we had in our budget for all schools. After three years of much welcomed NDS funding, the structural repair needs of our relatively small Authority still run at over £13 million.

There is little doubt that the introduction of *market forces* into schooling had a dramatic effect. Schools were encouraged to see themselves as mini-business units and many began to feel *isolated*. It is important to acknowledge some spectacular successes where individual institutions have become successful 'market leaders' and parental choice has been extended. But as always with markets there are losers as well as winners. There is no such thing as a perfect market, especially in the public sector, and it is clear that this market makes it difficult for the urban school to succeed. The dynamics of the school market place ensure that through a combination of the publication of exam results, OfSTED inspection, open enrolment and funding tied to pupils, even good schools in challenging areas struggle to survive. Schools with weaknesses face a potential spiral of decline in which poor published results leads to more aspiring parents moving themselves or their children elsewhere, budgets decline, the school becomes a net importer of excluded pupils from other schools, performance and image in the community is damaged further, it becomes harder to attract and retain staff and so on.

As with schools in our first box, in the worst cases some *local authorities* are *failing* to cope. They either lack appropriate leadership (at political or officer level), adequate strategies and skills or have simply been overwhelmed by the scale of the problems they face.

Economic and technological change

Surrounding these local conditions for schools and LEAs has been the rapid external changes which are affecting all services and societies. The spread of global capitalism across national boundaries and the resulting increased competition has had a dramatic impact on local economies and the likely skills and abilities needed for the future. The other related aspect of that change is the new technological revolution. The challenge for schools is to equip young people with the skills and attitudes for this rapidly changing world. The context in which learning takes place in the near future will undoubtedly be profoundly different.

Strategies for school improvement

Using the framework described above, it is possible to set out a range of strategies to tackle the challenges identified. (see Figure 8.2) We did not begin with this framework in Blackburn with Darwen and it would be wrong to suggest that our strategies were designed specifically to fit this model. Nevertheless it is possible to categorise many of our responses under these headings. In Blackburn with Darwen we established the phrase 'aiming high, including all' as our mission statement and this encapsulates the approach we have endeavoured to take.

THE STRATEGIES

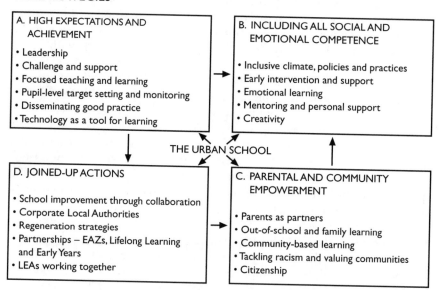

Figure 8.2 The strategies for urban schooling

High expectations and achievement

Crucial to this is leadership at LEA and school level. We have known for some time that leadership and management in schools is crucial. In urban schools this is even greater. For schools read also LEAs. LEAs need both professional and political leadership. Political leadership involves clarity and strength of agreement amongst key players about overall vision and goals and a policy framework within which officers can work. It is then important for politicians to give officers the space to get on with the task of achieving those goals, monitoring progress at regular but not too frequent intervals. As in all leadership the key is 'to understand more and interfere less' (Covey). Political leadership is tested most when faced with hard decisions which are politically difficult in the short term but clearly right for the long term goals. For professional leadership some of the same principles apply, in particular the need for a clear vision which is easily understood, collectively developed and owned by staff and schools. Knowledge and credibility are important, along with an ability to engage and enthuse staff in the LEA and schools to believe that real improvement is possible and then to make a difference and celebrate it.

Most LEAs are faced with some very difficult decisions. Building relationships with schools, developing an understanding of their concerns and needs and developing trust and confidence between officers, headteachers, governors and staff is therefore crucial. Whilst some LEAs are tempted to cus more on systems and procedures, it is essential to be absolutely committed to building relationships, developing a shared vision and nurturing a sense of belonging, within a community of schools. If LEAs are to be successful, it will be largely down to their face-to-face work with headteachers, teachers and governors.

The role of what is usually called the advisory or inspection service is now widely accepted as being crucial. In Blackburn with Darwen we decided to use the term 'School Improvement Officers'. This sent out a clear message that our expectations of the role would be different. The small team of School Improvement Officers does not try to carry out all of the roles traditionally done by LEA advisory/inspection services. They do not deliver INSET, carry out consultancy in schools or have a subject-specific specialism, with the exception of literacy and numeracy. Their work has a very clear focus around the following three interrelated strategies:

1 *Supporting school self-review and target setting* so that schools can more confidently make rigorous and evaluative judgements about themselves and be self-improving. The focus here has been on empowering schools, working alongside senior and middle-managers in looking together at their school and the teaching and learning within it.

2 *Help for schools causing concern and/or needing additional support.* The Authority was determined to focus additional support on these schools and to monitor their progress carefully. Considerable amounts of support have been provided and the success rate has been very high. At the time of writing the number of special measures schools has reduced from ten to one and there has been a similar success with those in serious weaknesses. Whilst there are no magic answers and each school in difficulty has its own unique features and needs a tailored approach, it is clear that certain types of strategy are more effective than others. As one of our headteachers whose school had been in serious weaknesses said: 'Coasting is impossible when you are being chased.'

3. *School improvement programmes.* These are fundamental to the Authority's strategy for school improvement. They involve schools working in a differentiated and focused way on improving teaching and learning and on raising achievement. The programmes also involve schools working in collaboration with each other so that good practice can be disseminated and ideas shared.

It is important that the clear focus of an LEA's school improvement work should be on making a difference in the classroom. The emphasis needs to be on helping schools to develop not just an understanding of good teaching and learning but the confidence and ability to articulate it and to discuss it professionally with colleagues in their own school and in other schools.

At secondary level the concept of *specialist schools* has a role to play in raising aspirations, tackling what might be a poor image of the school in the community, attracting new staff and additional, targeted resources. Specialist schools can also contribute to providing a more varied and relevant curriculum to meet the needs of a range of students. There is wide agreement that curriculum flexibility, at least at key stage 4, is an essential part of engaging all learners. In Blackburn with Darwen we now have three specialist schools in the LEA and have been proactive in supporting their applications. We hope, soon, to have two more and ultimately see no reason why we could not have a network involving all our schools.

From the start in Blackburn with Darwen, the Education Action Zone has been fully integrated into the work of the LEA, thus adding value to school improvement. The EAZ Director is also a member of the LEA's Senior Management Team and is fully involved in the strategic thinking across the LEA. Where schools are a cause for concern, the EAZ and the LEA work collaboratively to address the issues. There have been programmes in the EAZ to develop potential senior managers through the use of 360 degree appraisal methods, job shadowing in other schools and mentoring. The programme to improve teaching and learning has included the provision of focused support in literacy and in numeracy through subject-specialist teachers. These additional teachers spend up to a term in each school, working alongside teachers in classrooms and helping to develop literacy and numeracy teaching across the school.

Finally LEAs and schools need to grasp the opportunities which *Information and Communication Technology* offers to revolutionise our approach to learning. Having linked up all our schools we have moved on to a programme of training and support for schools to adapt their teaching styles and school organisation in the light of these developments in technology. In the EAZ the introduction of interactive whiteboards in all schools has led to a fundamental shift in how some teachers use technology in the classroom and has undoubtedly helped to motivate pupils and teachers. The interactive whiteboard has helped to ensure that all pupils in the class can use technology together at the same time, when in the past the use of computers has often been more of an isolated, individual activity. Through a product called the 'digital brain' all teachers and learners are to be given their own space on the web to develop and store teaching materials and the students' own work. The LEA's strategic role is to lead the development of ICT as a fundamental tool for learning.

Including all: Developing social and emotional competence

There are those who claim that raising standards and social inclusion are in conflict in schools. In Blackburn with Darwen we have stated our commitment to aiming high *and* including all. The LEA's leadership is crucial in this area, first, in establishing a *climate of inclusion* and being

epared to articulate why exclusion in all its forms is unacceptable and
ill have an impact not just on that school but society as a whole. The
LEA's role is as an advocate for all those young people at risk of exclusion
and as a guardian of equality of opportunity. Secondly, LEAs must be able
to provide practical help to schools in developing an inclusive culture in
which there are high expectations of all and every learner is accepted and
valued as an individual. We are working with other LEAs and with Professor Mel Ainscow and colleagues to support schools in developing *inclusive
policies and practices* which will respond to diversity and overcome the
barriers to learning and participation for all students (The teaching and
learning research programme, ESRC).

In this context it is important that LEA and school SEN policies are
about *early intervention and support* rather than assessment and categorisation. Pastoral and behaviour support programmes should be linked to
teaching and learning. This needs to be true at LEA level where the traditional role of advisers, in our case SIOs, must include a clear brief for supporting inclusive practices. The SIOs will be working to ensure that all
schools aim high and include all and will be monitoring and supporting
schools' progress in both. In Blackburn with Darwen we have set ambitious targets to reduce exclusions and have made rapid progress. Our
behaviour support plans include flexible provision and support for pupils
within and outside schools but always with high expectations for these
learners. Our SEN review devolved funds and responsibilities to schools
and sees the LEA's role to promote and monitor inclusive practices to meet
individual needs.

The earliest form of intervention is through the early years curriculum
and we have put a strong emphasis on access for all to high-quality early
years provision.

Goleman identifies a curriculum response by promoting the explicit
teaching and learning of *emotional literacy*. Some schools, faced with difficult and disturbed youngsters, have simply taken the view that they need
to be a 'caring' school: listening to pupils and parents and providing
general support inside and outside schools. We would not want to belittle
this approach but there is a need to have more specific and rigorous
strategies.

Goleman's curriculum is about 'harmonising the heart and the head'
and promoting emotional as well as intellectual intelligence. His curriculum includes self-awareness, managing emotions, motivation, empathy and
handling relationships. Goleman provides evidence that 'emotional com-
petences can be taught and learned ... emotional literacy programmes
improve children's academic achievement scores and school performance'
(1996: 284).

It would be wrong to claim that in Blackburn with Darwen we have
gone very far with this approach as yet but in partnership with others we
have started. In the EAZ we have established pyramid clubs, working with

the National Pyramid Trust, which explicitly address the development of 'resilience and self-esteem' and the 'emotional health' of young people at risk. Nurture groups have been established in schools where behaviour has become a particular challenge. All our high schools now have 'in-school centres' which typically include staff with counselling skills. As part of a major SEN review we are looking to redirect the work of the educational psychology service away from the crazy bureaucracy of statement chasing to allow them to spend more time on proactive, preventative work of this kind.

In schools aspects of the emotional curriculum can be organised in many ways, whether within PSHE or Citizenship or as part of the pastoral curriculum and support systems. Out of school learning also provides a range of new opportunities for tackling this kind of work with those most in need. Our summer learning programme, known as 'Summer Slam', attracted a wide range of youngsters including some looked after children and others at risk. We have plans to develop this further in future years. We are also, through the Youth Service, developing Adventure Learning Programmes for potentially disaffected pupils, funded through SRB. In addition, many of our secondary schools and some of our primary schools already have school councils and we are looking at ways of further developing this so that young people feel that they are real stakeholders in the learning process in their school.

There is now growing evidence that some (possibly all) pupils benefit from another significant other, adult or peer, in the form of a *mentor to provide personal support*. The role can include listening, supporting, encouraging, monitoring progress and linking home and school. In our EAZ we have appointed 'pupil support mentors' in each school, recruited from the local community and given intensive training and support. Not only does this provide mentors for those young people most at risk of underachieving or being excluded but it contributes to capacity building for the community. This is supplemented by volunteer mentors from local businesses and in future will include peer mentors, partly provided by local colleges. Nationally this programme will be expanded via Excellence in Cities and Connexions.

Finally, we have provided opportunities for the *creative stimulation* of young people within and outside schools. The concept of creativity, as captured in the Robinson Report, is one we aim to embrace across all our work. Certainly our early years curriculum has an intensive focus in this area. However, we have also commissioned some explicit projects around 'creative citizenship'. In the EAZ, two drama companies are working with schools and the community to develop workshops and performances on the theme of citizenship. The brief has included training up members of the local community so that the capacity for community arts is developed alongside the skills and creative abilities of young people. As one of our headteachers put it, 'we need to give some of these children the experience of joy in their lives before they can really go on to learn and grow as human beings'.

Parental and community empowerment

The factors that lead to unstable communities require strategies well beyond the role of schools and LEAs. They are driven by the global economic and technological forces described above and influenced at best by Government policy at the highest level. Nevertheless, Local Authorities have their role to play in responding to poor housing and family breakdown and, over and above these factors, LEAs and schools can work together to engage and empower parents and communities.

We have often failed to see parents as the key partners in this process. Until recently teachers have often wanted to keep parents at a distance – promoting the idea of the detached professional, fearful of interfering or challenging parents.

Andy Hargreaves has written about three stages of engaging parents and communities; beginning with parents helping their children's education, then parents learning themselves and finally teachers being prepared to learn from parents. Hargreaves believes we need an alliance of teachers and parents if we are to bring about the educational changes required (Hargreaves and Fullan, 1998).

In Blackburn with Darwen we have tried a number of approaches to *involve and engage parents as partners*. The 'parents as educators' programme, begun with Lancashire LEA and extended and developed in our EAZ, has had a profound impact. Parents with poor experiences of school have developed new skills and greater confidence and self-esteem. The programme has simultaneously developed the parent's own learning as well as their ability to support their child's education. Many of the parents have gone on to enrol in further accredited learning and in some cases to jobs as pupil support mentors within the zone.

Out of school learning opportunities have been used to attract both parents and children. We have *family learning* programmes in literacy, numeracy, ICT and the arts and our summer schools have included opportunities for the whole family, including grandparents to engage in learning. The Mustard Seed House 'Roots Project' in the EAZ aims to provide outreach support for families in crisis. A summer scheme is planned aimed specifically at single fathers and their children.

This is where the LEAs' leadership of lifelong and community learning comes into its own. We have developed a number of *community-based learning centres*, some in schools but others not. As primary schools begin to develop computer suites these provide an ideal, non-threatening atmosphere for parents and teachers to learn ICT skills together – recognising that in this area it is often the child that knows most! This is what Tim Brighouse has termed the 'home and community curriculum'. It is about valuing and engaging the community in a cultural change about the who, how, when and where of learning. Our motto for this work is 'life is all about learning'.

Tackling racism is a huge task in its own right. At the very least, LEAs and schools need to engage with ethnic minority communities on their terms. They need to listen and understand and then develop strategies as an integral part of their approach to inclusion. In Blackburn with Darwen we have made a start but still have a long way to go. We have commissioned research into the views of ethnic minority parents and young people. We are extending our ethnic monitoring and support for target setting as part of a specific programme for raising ethnic minority achievement. We also have homework centres focused on our ethnic communities and are working with some local mosques to develop out of school learning partnerships. We have an anti-bullying forum in which all high schools share their data, policies and practices on tackling bullying and racial harassment.

The new *citizenship* curriculum also provides opportunities in this area. Not the dry civics of institutions but active citizenship in which young people develop skills through direct involvement in the community. In the EAZ we have used artists to work with children and adults to create sculptures, dramas and environmental landscapes. Through the Youth Service and out of school programmes as well as within schools we are encouraging young people to become involved in making decisions about the provision that is for them. And through the creation of Community Regeneration Zones we are taking steps to enable local people begin to engage in shaping the policies and programmes for their communities.

Partnerships and collaborations

The challenges facing public services require two main types of response. The first is to ensure that those services in the public sector are working collaboratively together and maximising effectiveness and impact. The second is to seek out other partners in the private and voluntary sectors.

At school level the first of these involves *collaboration for school improvement* including disseminating good practice, learning from and with each other and challenging each other. School Improvement Programmes, with their emphasis on sharing and collaboration, are at the heart of what we do in Blackburn with Darwen. From their Development Plan and self-review the school chooses their main priority for the year to work on to improve teaching and learning and to raise standards. Schools are grouped into networks to share experiences and meet three times a year with the support of the LEA. Schools also attend a day conference and send a small team to a residential conference to learn more about school improvement and to share practice. A newsletter of case studies and outcomes from these projects is produced at the end of the year in order to share and disseminate good practice.

In addition, we have developed Benchmark Learning Groups for Head-teachers. Under this arrangement headteachers from similar schools meet together with senior officers from the LEA to discuss, honestly, the successes and the problems in their schools and to share ideas for addressing common concerns. Each termly session is followed by a 'homework' which always involves working collaboratively with another headteacher on a common issue and reporting back to the next meeting.

Most important of all has been the partnership and collaboration across schools that has been increasingly evident in the LEA as schools have been prepared to put themselves out to help other schools. Time after time headteachers and governors have been prepared to release their own staff to support another school in difficulty. Such support and collaboration from schools has been outstanding, considering the immense pressures and accountability every school is under, even good schools.

Inter-school collaboration is at the heart of the EAZ. Schools in the zone work together in each of the programme areas including teaching and learning, management and leadership, creative citizenship and early years. In one particular initiative we are exploring the single management of two schools with governing bodies ceding powers to the zone who then establish a new joint body. Outside Blackburn with Darwen, Excellence in Cities offers a further development of this approach, whereby secondary schools operate with small clusters of primaries as mini-EAZs.

Within the LEA one of the key challenges is to ensure the various teams and sections of the *Education Department* are *working together to support and challenge schools*. In Blackburn with Darwen this has been a high priority and one of the key reasons why we have been successful. Individuals from services across the department have met together, on a number of occasions, to develop a coherent and focused support programme for particular schools in difficulty. We also have an annual joint review of all schools involving all parts of the department. Without that joined-up working it would have been far more difficult to address the range of complex issues that schools in difficulty invariably face.

In Blackburn with Darwen structures and processes have been designed to support *corporate working* – including the appointment of executive directors without departmental responsibilities whose task is to enable joined up working. In reality however, what makes this work is more about culture and personal relationships than structures. Examples of this in practice include the joint work with social services over looked after children and families in need; with community, leisure and culture over out of school learning opportunities; and with a number of departments on strategies to tackle social exclusion. Perhaps most crucially we have sought to place education at the heart of our regeneration strategies. Regeneration has too often been solely about inward investment and the physical infrastructure but our strategy is about people; with informal education, training for skills and capacity building in communities as key elements. In the light of the economic and technological changes referred to above it is crucial that strategies to modernise and diversify the local economy go hand in hand with the development of new skills and outlooks for local people – otherwise when the jobs are created it is people from outside who will come in to fill them leaving an even more excluded local community.

Partnership is a much used word these days. Sometimes the reality is little more than marriages of convenience to attract funding. If a real impact is to made on the problems highlighted above then it is genuine joint working that matters, where the whole is greater than the sum of the parts. This involves, for example, local authorities accepting that the voluntary sector is often best placed to deliver work with families and communities. More controversially it means acknowledging that in some cases, for a specific service, the private sector are the best providers and for others a partnership between public and private. What is important is the terms under which those partnerships are developed and the need to retain safeguards for democratic accountability. However, out-sourcing itself is not, in our view, the answer as it cannot meet the need for multi-faceted approaches and joined up strategies. Take for example the case of an individual school in difficulty. This school may need support at management and leadership level, improved capacity on the governing body, personnel advice to handle underperformance, improved literacy teaching, better marketing to the community, more support for parents facing poverty and poor housing. It is unlikely that the private sector can deliver on this range of needs in a co-ordinated way. The big question is, can the public sector cope? The answer is probably not on its own but if it is close to that community, it probably has the best chance of understanding the needs and facilitating a range of partners to provide, including its own education department.

New forms of partnership have emerged in recent years to demonstrate the power of working together across sectors. In our case the *EAZ, a Lifelong Learning Forum and Partnership and the Early Years Development and Childcare Partnership* have each provided new opportunities and creative solutions to complex local issues.

Finally we are beginning to see *LEAs working together* in new and imaginative ways. As a new unitary we teamed up with the City of Nottingham, a statistical neighbour and unitary of the same age. We have appeared at each other's conferences, exchanged ideas and information, undertaken work-shadowing, reviewed each other's services and established links between headteachers. Through our Beacon status we have worked with other LEAs and the LEA is now involved in an innovative partnership with Rochdale LEA to support their improvement plan. We are bringing our experience of starting a new LEA to this work but are also keen to learn for ourselves from these partnerships. We are convinced there are considerable further opportunities and benefits in this way of working. The business of school improvement is complex and specialised. By and large the people with the skills and knowledge in this area are in LEAs, a few universities and of course in schools. We need to find ways to maximise the use and development of these skills through joint working, exchanges and staff development opportunities.

Using the framework

Although we have presented the dimensions of this framework as separate they are of course interrelated and the interaction between the strategies is crucial to their impact. For example, there is no doubt that good teaching can motivate and that success itself can raise self-esteem thus improving emotional competence. Learning in the community will have an impact on regeneration. Partnerships such as EAZs can add value (or, if misdirected, create barriers) to school improvement. An improving school can help to lift the image and esteem of a community. Part of the role of the LEA is to be aware of the possibilities and enable these positive interactions to occur.

It is our view that the dimensions in the framework are all important although not necessarily equally so for all partners – it is largely a matter of balance. The activities of OfSTED, for example, have concentrated almost exclusively on the top left dimension of the framework, at times appearing to deny the relevance of the rest. The impact of social, emotional and community factors are undeniable to anyone who has taught in challenging urban schools. If schools and LEAs do not have strategies to tackle the barriers to learning and engage their communities then progress against hard academic targets will be limited. Equally, however, schools that use the reality of poverty as a reason for low expectations and a lack of rigour in teaching and the curriculum are doing a profound disservice to the young people and the community they claim to serve. Poverty has a real impact on schools but it does not make their task impossible – it makes it harder and it requires more support, including from the LEA.

Michael Barber has referred to the power of 'and' rather than 'or' in tackling these issues. There is no single magic solution or strategy to secure successful urban schooling. What is needed is a balanced approach which tackles the challenges on each of the dimensions in our framework. Goleman recognises this in his work when he writes, 'To be sure, the causes of all such problems are complex, interweaving different ratios of biological destiny, family dynamics, the politics of poverty and the culture of the streets. No single kind of intervention, including one targeting emotions, can claim to do the whole job. But to the degree emotional deficits add to a child's risk, attention must be paid to emotional remedies, not to the exclusion of other answers but along with them' (Goleman, 1996: 260). The same could be said of all the dimensions discussed in this article.

This is where the role of the LEA should come into its own. It is our view that the LEA is best placed to take a strategic view of this process – to ensure all the dimensions have been considered and to monitor and continually adjust the balance. However, it is emphatically not for the LEA to do it all themselves. Some of these activities clearly need to be driven by schools with LEAs in a monitoring and supporting role, intervening where necessary but not too much. Some are the role of other Government agencies and the private and voluntary sectors. But in the end there is a need for a local organisation, rooted in and accountable to the community, to identify the challenges and co-ordinate the strategies. This is not to suggest that this is an easy task nor that LEAs are all up to that task. However, we believe they are best placed to do so and that in Blackburn with Darwen we have at least made a start. In September 2000 OfSTED inspected Blackburn with Darwen and the Report described the work on school inprovement as 'outstanding' and judged that there had already been 'a marked impact on raising standards'. The authority was judged as 'a most effective LEA'. The task for all LEAs is to improve their capacity to take on these challenges and to learn from each other and from other partners. The nature of these challenges is such that top-down solutions are unlikely to make much progress and that change must be generated from within the communities concerned. LEAs should be at the heart of that change.

9 The way forward

New model LEAs for the twenty-first century

David Woods and Martyn Cribb

> The question we have to ask ourself is not whether an education authority should exist – I have said before that if we didn't have authorities we would have to invent something similar. Rather, it is in what form and for which century.
>
> David Blunkett, Speech, 11 May 2000

> It should be possible now, as never before, to draw on the expertise which exists in the community, between Authorities and in other public, voluntary and private sector organisations to achieve the object of an excellent education for all children.
>
> (*The Role of the LEA in School Education*, DfEE, October 2000)

This book has examined effective LEAs and school improvement and the ways in which LEAs can make a difference to the raising of educational standards. We know that LEAs are well placed to support schools through extensive local knowledge and considerable expertise and experience in managing services that support school improvement. We also know that LEAs cannot control schools but can influence them through effective consultation, partnership, support, challenge and leadership enhancing the school's own capacity to sustain improvement and *intervening* in inverse proportion to success. As Liz Allen comments in her pamphlet on *Future Models of Local Education* (2000), 'Local education authorities, with their duty to promote high standards, have a duty to help schools to fly' and to do this they require a range of externally provided services and support. Yet LEAs are about community needs as well as school needs and about raising education achievement for all individuals and groups within the community.

Through OfSTED and Audit Commission inspection evidence of some three-fifths of LEAs we have a range of evidence about what constitutes poor or good LEAs and that LEAs range in their support for school improvement from the excellent to those that are very ineffective. In their report on *Local Education Authority Support for School Improvement* OfSTED and the Audit Commission have identified particular characteristics of highly effective LEAs.

- clear definitions of monitoring, challenge, intervention and support which are reflected in the targeting of resources;
- the application of best value to services with no predilection for either the public or the private sector;
- effective consultation with stakeholders leading to high trust;
- the management of multi-agency working at strategic and operational level – effective partnerships and synergy;
- a strategy for, and the ability to, enhance the school's own capacity to sustain continuous improvement.

Whilst these are useful criteria and challenges for new model LEAs they still allow for a range of practices and interpretations particularly when one considers the different types of LEAs (County, Unitary and Metropolitan) ranging in size from one school to over 700. These LEAs will offer different models and applications whilst building effective partnerships with schools and stakeholders which do lead to high-trust and build capacity for improvement. Certainly the importance of a high trust culture emerges time and time again from the research evidence.

Changing Partners (Audit Commission, 1998) stressed the importance of the LEAs' community leadership role to meet the diverse needs of learners in their localities working with local partnerships, and the complexity of interrelationships:

> An LEA is more than a series of processes, decisions and information flows. It is also a bundle of personal interactions, behaviours and feelings which require at least as much management attention. Even the best organisational systems will fail to generate improvement unless accompanied by a series of less tangible attributes that encourage staff in the authority and schools to feel motivated and valued, understand what they should be doing, work together constructively and give enthusiastically of their best.

Kathryn Riley in her contribution to *What Makes a Good LEA?* (TEN, 2000) entitled 'Bottling the Ingredients of Success' refers to a climate of momentum, enthusiasm and trust sustained by clear professional leadership, about what can be achieved and how, and a 'working with you' approach. The Roehampton project, begun in late 1995 on 'The Changing Role and Effectiveness of LEAs' has assessed the effectiveness of eighteen LEAs to date and the central conclusion is that LEAs can make a significant contribution to their local education community.

What seems to matter is *how* LEAs go about their business: how they create a climate of continuous improvement and an urgency for change, and how they link resources to agreed objectives. The 'how' is about ethos: the expectations and aspirations and the ways in which

things are done which can bind an education community together –
the absence of which can fragment it.

(*What Makes a Good LEA?* TEN, 2000)

The recent NFER study on *The LEA Contribution to School Improvement*
(July 2000) similarly stressed the importance of processes (of service
delivery and the building of partnerships) in having a positive impact on
outputs. The study identified a number of features that would facilitate
effective processes:

- empowerment to help LEAs influence the nature and extent of changing schools;
- awareness of what schools actually want from their LEAs;
- agreement about what LEAs can and cannot reasonably be expected
  to provide for schools;
- time and adequate opportunities for LEAs to develop effective partnerships with schools;
- knowledge of schools and their context in order for link advisers to
  challenge them effectively;
- trust and mutual respect between link advisers and headteachers; and
- acknowledgement of the wide-ranging LEA support that goes 'behind
  the scenes'.

The picture that emerges from the evidence generally and the studies in
this book is complex with a rapidly changing policy context within the
current agendas of modernising local government, best value, social inclusion, economic regeneration and community safety. Within these corporate
themes LEAs need to secure a wide range of educational services encom-
passing early years education, education at school, community education
and lifelong learning and manage the transitions between these sectors.
The LEA also manages or contributes to local partnerships with further
education and higher education, learning and skills councils, the business community, local dioceses, and sometimes EAZ and EiC groupings.
Central government has given LEAs a new statutory duty to raise standards and increased their accountability through the effective implementation of Education Development Plans, and achieving performance targets
at KS2 and KS4 and for improving attendance, reducing exclusions, and
improving the achievement of looked after children. As well as increased
accountability to the DfEE, LEAs are also subject to inspection from
OfSTED and the Audit Commission. Against this background *Held in
Trust* (Audit Commission, 1999) points out 'the government has made it
clear that an LEA's successes will be judged largely in terms of the educational performance of its schools. School improvement is therefore central
to the future of LEAs'. Yet LEAs can only seek to influence the drive
and methods to improve standards through a combination of support and

challenge working at arm's length unless schools are causing concern where they do have reserve powers.

The central question therefore is, given these constraints, what do effective LEAs do to secure school improvement? Martin Rogers, the co-ordinator of the Education Network, in his article on 'Reinventing the LEA' (*Education Journal*, June 2000) states that

> the main requirements are to improve the quality of teaching and learning: to raise aspiration as well as achievement (especially amongst groups where levels of either are traditionally low); to generate, identify, develop and disseminate best practice; to recruit, train and retrain sufficiently high quality staff; to maximise the benefits to be derived from co-ordinating the inputs of all agencies whose work has a bearing on educational outcomes; and to make the best possible use of funds in the provision and utilisation of learning opportunities ... such good, habits, once established, will then be turned to maintaining the high standards achieved.

In *The Role of the LEA in School Education* (DfEE, 2000), the government suggests four further ways of building on Fair Funding and reinforcing the modernising agenda:

- helping to promote a more open market in school services and taking steps to ensure that all schools have the skills to operate Best Value principles;
- sharing school improvement responsibilities with groups of schools;
- develop and trial new ways of discharging responsibility in partnership with other LEAs and the public, private and voluntary sector;
- helping to develop national professional standards and national recognition of those engaged in the key role of school improvement.

The many case studies, small and large, referred to in this book show how effective LEAs have developed and are developing particular *habits* in their efforts to support school improvement and raise standards.

Stephen Covey, in his book on *The 7 Habits of Highly Effective People* (1994), defines habits as the intersections of knowledge, skill and desire and comments that habits 'provide an incremental, sequential, highly integrated approach to the development of polite and interpersonal effectiveness'. The same holds true for organisational effectiveness and the following are seven habits of highly effective LEAs in supporting school improvement:

- leadership, sharing values and reinforcing a common language of improvement;
- a relentless press to raise standards both in school performance and local services;
- building partnerships, trust and capacity;

- gathering, disseminating and using performance data;
- enhancing the school's capacity for self review and self improvement;
- monitoring, challenging, reviewing, supporting and intervening in inverse proportion to success; and
- promoting and disseminating good practice.

Leadership, sharing values and reinforcing a common language of improvement

LEAs sit at the centre of learning communities and should provide an overall vision and strategic overview of school improvement and the raising of educational standards. They should be in the habit of responding to local needs as well as national priorities. This may be seen through the LEAs overall strategic plan as well as the Education Development Plan in particular which will articulate shared values and beliefs. These may relate to ways of working with reference to the habits and processes of consultation, mutuality, collegiality and networking as well as fostering shared beliefs relating to such issues as social inclusion, equal opportunities and the rights and interests of individuals and groups. The practising of these processes will lead to a high trust LEA which will engender a common drive to work together to raise standards.

A relentless press to raise standards both in school performance and local services

There are clear indicators of success for both LEAs and schools in terms of raising standards of achievement. The government has, through the EDP, negotiated targets to raise standards at Key Stage 2 and Key Stage 4 as well as improving attendance, reducing exclusions, and improving the performance of looked after children. Other targets may be part of Excellence in Cities partnerships, EAZs or locally agreed objectives. The relentless press may be in applying challenge and support to schools in setting and getting their targets, or in improving low performing schools, or in working collectively to improve the standards of under achieving groups of children and young people. The LEA needs to help create an infrastructure to support learning both in and out of school but also with its schools maintain the highest of expectations. Similarly in terms of improving local services an effective LEA will be in the habit of benchmarking its provision against other services, operating Best Value principles, setting up a rolling programme of service reviews and district audit surveys.

Building partnerships, trust and capacity

As we have seen from the various case studies in this book, LEAs can work with a wide range of partners to help them raise standards and be a catalyst for learning. Trust and mutual respect is unlikely to be achieved without regular consultation and agreed ways of working. Apart from schools who are the principal partners of LEAs, there are sets of standard partnerships, established in most LEAs – Early Years, Education and Business, Lifelong Learning, TECs and for some Excellence in Cities and Education Action Zones.

There are also sets of informal partnerships – with parents, community groups, young people, further and higher education and a wider range of public, voluntary and private sector partners already engaged in education who might work with LEAs. The partnership habit is about getting the best out of each other for the benefit of all and most particularly schools and their students. Good partnership habits practised by effective LEAs involve:

- collaborative working
- the encouragement and recognition of success
- trust and mutual respect
- shared accountability.

Gathering, disseminating and using performance data

LEAs need to continually strive to provide a wide range of benchmarking data in order to support and challenge schools more effectively and to assist schools in self-evaluation. As all schools already have access to national performance and benchmarking data including PANDAs, LEAs need to add value through:

- a sophisticated range of contextual data;
- benchmarking data of 'like' schools;
- establishing pupil tracking systems through individual pupil data bases;
- electronic communication systems;
- providing a responsive service to the queries and concerns of individual schools with reference to performance data; and
- an ongoing training and support service in 'data fluency' for schools and governors.

Further, through the use of the LEA profile provided by OfSTED and the collection of other evidence, LEAs should be in the habit of benchmarking their own performance against their statistical neighbours.

Supporting teaching and learning, leadership and management through continuous professional development

LEAs have a clear strategic role in supporting teaching and learning and developing leadership and management but the models of support and delivery may vary significantly depending upon capacity. All LEAs, through their Education Development Plans and the Standards Fund will offer some 'in-house' professional development. However, this is not always a matter of direct provision but sometimes one of *brokerage* – putting schools in touch with accredited external providers or acting as a *facilitator* – enabling regular meetings of practitioners to take place.

In their strategic role effective LEAs will supplement the best efforts of their schools through *co-ordination* – bringing together partners to provide particular INSET opportunities. Clearly the TTA, GTC, QCA, OfSTED and the DfEE have something to contribute to continuous professional development – LEAs can help schools make sense of the various opportunities presented by these bodies.

Monitoring, challenging, reviewing, supporting and intervening in inverse proportion to success

The key issue here is the habit of differentiating support levels for schools with the capacity to make finely tuned adjustments as schools either improve or decline. The smart LEA will have advanced intelligence systems to enable it to make appropriate interventions. It will be able to call up a considerable range of performance data, use the best benchmarking techniques and come to a judgement on the progress of its schools. It will supplement this by reference to OfSTED Inspection evidence and its own fieldwork evidence on such qualitative issues as the quality of relationships, ethos, and the effectiveness of leadership and management. It will have a highly trained, expert advisory service with the skills to operate as both a critical friend and a change agent and challenge appropriately.

Generating, identifying, promoting and disseminating good practice

There is a danger of schools becoming inward looking and an isolated school is probably a coasting or declining school. As this study has shown LEAs are in an ideal position to identify, broker, develop and network good practice. However, to achieve this there is a need for LEAs to be proactive in developing an appropriate strategy in consultation with schools, shared by the learning community they represent and taking advantage of their extensive, local knowledge. Good LEAs will not only bring practitioners and schools together but also commission particular projects based on an audit of local needs and harness good practice from the private and voluntary sectors. The habits of LEAs who are best at promoting good practice are around development, identification and connection but of course, good practice also needs to be quality assured to see that it can be applied in various settings and be sustainable over time if it is to make a significant impact on raising standards.

LEAs will need to be very sensitive to the needs and expectations of their schools and stakeholders as well as having the confidence to challenge effectively to raise standards of achievement. Perhaps the role of the effective LEA in making a difference to school improvement can be summed up as follows:

- *providing* an overarching vision and leadership of a learning community;
- *maintaining* effective consultation and relationships;
- *sharing* school improvement responsibilities with groups of schools;
- *building* trust and capacity through partnerships and the management of multi-agency working;
- *applying* best value and benchmarking of multi-agency working to all services;
- *discharging* responsibilities in partnership with other LEAs and with other public, private and voluntary bodies;
- *creating*, school leadership and governor development opportunities;
- *making* interconnections between innovations;
- *identifying* and *disseminating* good practice;
- *monitoring* and supporting school effectiveness and improvement;
- *supporting* school self-evaluation and development planning;
- *providing* performance data to inform and sustain school improvement;
- *helping* to set targets and get targets to raise standards of achievement; and
- *intervening* appropriately to secure improvement.

The evidence shows that well run LEAs with these habits do have a positive impact on the work of schools and in raising the standards of achievement of children and young people. Raising standards of achievement is at the heart of the work of the LEA. Central to this is the raising of aspirations as well of achievement and the identification and elimination of failure or underperformance of particular groups of pupils. Current attention is focused on the relatively poor performance of boys in comparison to girls and the underperformance of certain minority ethnic groups. The underachievement of these groups is a national phenomenon but through local working with schools, parents and communities it is likely that improvements will be made. It is here that the LEA is well placed to make a difference and to co-ordinate the work of a number of agencies and departments to deliver high quality services to tackle localised failure or underperformance.

Schools have frontline responsibility for raising standards and key to this is the LEA's support for self-improvement in all schools which focuses attention upon the quality of teaching and learning as well as the quality of leadership and management. Effective LEAs are able to monitor, support, challenge and intervene appropriately and to facilitate collaboration and networking so that good practice can be shared or to broker further support. They work successfully with a range of partners in the public, voluntary and private sectors so that they can secure the best services for their schools.

In a broader context local authorities are well placed to promote social inclusion and tackle the deprivation of local communities. The many initiatives aimed at addressing deprivation – New Deal for Community, Single Regeneration, Funding, Community Plans, Neighbourhood Renewal, Surestart etc. place the Local Authority at the head of the drive to improve opportunities. The LEA is central to the joining up and delivery of this broad agenda. LEAs are the custodians of education for local people. Local democratic control, well run and administered, adds considerably to the quality of debate and breath of understanding of what is needed to provide the best education for local people in a national context.

Bibliography

Allen, L., *Future Models of Local Education*, New Local Government Network (2000)

Arnold, R., *Education Development Plans: Meeting targets and improving schools* (EMIE Report 51) NFER (1999)

Arnold, R., *Schools, LEAs and University: the improvement of schools through partnership*, NFER (1995)

Audit Commission, *Assuring Quality in Education – audit role of LEA inspectors and advisers* (1989)

Audit Commission, *Changing Partners: a discussion paper on the role of the LEA* (1998)

Audit Commission, *Held in Trust, the LEA of the Future* (1999)

Audit Commission, *Losing an Empire, Finding a Role: the LEA of the future* (1989)

Bangs, J., *LEAs and Schools: a social partnership*, TEN (1998)

Barber, M., *The Learning Game*, Victor Gollancz (1996)

Barber, M. and Turner, J., 'Recognising LEA Effectiveness', in M. Rogers (ed.) *What Makes a Good LEA?*, TEN (2000)

Bird, S., *The Government Inspectors Call*, TEN (1999)

Bird, S., *Who Does What?*, TEN (1999)

Bird, S., *Adding Value to School Improvement*, TEN (2000)

Brighouse, T. and Woods, D.C., *How to Improve Your School*, Routledge (1999)

Clark, D., *Schools as Learning Communities*, Cassell (1996)

Covey, Stephen, *The Seven Habits of Highly Effective People*, Simon & Schuster (1994)

Dean, J., *Inspecting and Advising*, Routledge (1992)

Derington, C., *LEAs and School Improvement – a role worth fighting for*, NFER (July 2000)

DfEE, *Building Professional Knowledge (LEA Contribution to Good Practice)*, (2000)

DfEE, *Code of Practice on LEA–School Relations* (1998, revised 2000)

DfEE, *Connecting the Learning Society – the National Grid for Learning* (1997)

DfEE, *Excellence for All Children: meeting special educational needs* (1997)

DfEE, *Excellence in Cities*, (1999)

DfEE, *Excellence in Schools* (1997)

DfEE, *EDP Guidance* (1998) and *New Guidance on EDPs* (November 2000)

DfEE, *Fair Funding – improving delegation to schools* (1998)

DfEE, *From Targets to Action* (1997)

DfEE, *The Governor's Role in Raising Standards* (1998)

DfEE, *Guidance on Good Governance* (1996)

DfEE, *Meet the Challenge – Education Action Zones* (1998)

DfEE, *Modernising Local Government Finance* (2000)

DfEE, *Professional Development – support for teaching and learning* (2000)

DfEE, *Pupil Support and Social Exclusion* (1998)

DfEE, *Raising Aspirations in the 21st Century* (2000)

DfEE, *The Role of the LEA in School Education* (October 2000)

DfEE, *Schools Building on Success* (February 2001)

DfEE, *Schools Plus: building learning communities* (2000)

DfEE, *Targets to Action – guidance to support effective target setting* (1997)

DfEE, *Transforming Secondary Education* – pamphlet of a speech by David Blunkett to the Social Market Foundation (March 2000)

DfEE/OfSTED, *Setting Targets to Raise Standards* (1996)

DETR, *Modern Local Government: in touch with the people* (1998)

DETR, *Report on Beacon Councils* (November 1999)

Docking, J. (ed.), *National School Policy*, David Fulton (1996)

Docking, J. (ed.), *New Labour's Policies for Schools*, David Fulton (2000)

Fullan, M.G., *The New Meaning of Educational Change*, Cassell (1991)

Fullan, M.G., *Successful School Improvement*, Open University Press (1992)

Gann, N., *Improving School Governance*, Falmer Press (1998)

Goleman, D., *Emotional Intelligence*, Bloomsbury (1996)

Goodwin, S., *The Wider Role for Education*, TEN (1998)

Gray, J. *Causing Concern but Improving: a review of schools' experiences* (March 2000)

Handy, C., *The Age of Unreason*, Arrow (1995)

Handy, C., *Beyond Certainty: the changing world of organisations,* Arrow (1996)

Hargreaves, D., *Creative Professionalism: the role of the teachers in the knowledge society, DEMOS* (1998)

Hargreaves, D., and Fullan, M.G., *What's Worth Fighting for in Education?*, Open University Press (1998)

Hendy, J., *The New LEAs*, NFER (2000)

Hopkins, D., Ainscow, M. and West, M., *School Improvement in an Era of Change*, Cassell (1994)

Hopkins D. and Hargreaves D., *The Empowered School,* Cassell (1991)

Joyce, B., Calhoun, E. and Hopkins, D., *The New Structure of School Improvement*, Open University Press (1999)

LGA, *Has the LEA had its day?* (July 2000)

LGA, Part of the Solution – perspectives on the future educational role of the local authority (1999)

McMahon, A. and Bolam, R., *A Handbook for LEAs*, Paul Chapman (1990)

National Commission on Education, *Success Against the Odds*, Routledge, (1996)

NFER, *The LEA Contribution to School Improvement* (2000)

OfSTED, *From Failure to Success* (1997)

OfSTED, *Improving City Schools* (2000)

OfSTED, *HMCI Annual Reports* (1998–1999) and (1999–2000)

OfSTED, *LEA Support for School Improvement: framework for the inspection of LEAs* (1999)

OfSTED, *Local Education Authority Support for School Improvement* (February 2001)
OfSTED, *Making Headway* (1998)
OfSTED, *Lessons Learned from Special Measures* (1998)
OfSTED/SEU, *School Evaluation Matters* (1998)
O'Keefe, J., *Business Beyond the Box,* Nicholas Brealey (1999)
Ranson, S., *The Role of Local Government in Education,* Longman (1992)
Ribbins, P. and Burridge, E., *Improving Education, Promoting Quality in Schools,* Cassell (1994)
Riley, K., *Whose School Is it Anyway?,* Falmer Press (1998)
Roger, M., 'Reinventing the LEA', *Education Journal,* 46: 10 June 2000)
Rogers, M. (ed.), *What Makes a Good LEA?,* TEN (2000)
Russell, S., *Collaborative School Self- Review* Lemos & Krane (1996)
Whitbourn, S., Mitchell, K. and Morris, R., *What is the LEA For?,* NFER (2000)
Woods, D.C. (ed.), *School Improvement Butterflies,* Questions Publishing (1997)
Woods, D.C., *The Promotion and Dissemination of Good Practice, A Key Task for LEAs,* The Education Network, (November 2000)

Index

www.routledgefalmer.com

Last year saw the merging of two of the major names in education publishing, Falmer Press and Routledge Education. This new imprint now provides an unrivalled selection of education books and journals, from the practical to the academic and from student textbooks to high level research. We see this merger as an exciting moment in the history of both companies.

The RoutledgeFalmer Resource Centre is an ideal source of information of all kinds for those of you working in education. Whether you are a teacher, student, headteacher, lecturer, governor or you work for an education-related organisation, this site will prove of great use to you, containing comprehensive information on:

- books
- journals
- links to related sites
- essential textbooks for your course
- key new and forthcoming titles
- information for authors or contributors to our journals.

the *name for*
education books

Leadership for Change

International Perspectives on
Relational Leadership

Edited by

Kathryn Riley and Karen Seashore Louis

This book offers a rich comparative perspective on leadership. It examines the global influences, the differing national and state contexts which shape leadership, the impact of local pressures and priorities, as well as how leadership is exercised within schools themselves.

The contributors are leading researchers from Australia, Denmark, Canada, England, Scotland, the US and Wales and have a deep understanding of both policy and practice. Their invaluable insights enable the reader to understand the extent to which leadership is bound in context – local and national – as well as influenced by global and national trends.

August 2000: 234 × 156mm: 208pp.
Hb: 0-415-22792-5: £50.00
Pb: 0-415-22793-3: £16.99

Schools Must Speak for Themselves

The Case for School Self-Evaluation

John MacBeath

'Improvement occurs when people are not put on the defensive. It starts with questions in your mind about what you are doing and it accelerates when you share them with others engaged in the same enterprise. This book provides the questions and the means to accelerate improvement. It's a must for those serious about successful schooling.' – *Professor Tim Brighouse, Chief Education Officer at Birmingham City Council.*

'This is a work that speaks to teachers in a voice that suggests it understands what their job entails and the support they need. I found it hard to put down ... A worthwhile addition to any Inset library!' – *Managing Schools Today*

This best-selling book illustrates how schools can tell their own story. It draws on ground-breaking work with the National Union of teachers to demonstrate a practical approach to identifying what makes a good school and the part that pupils, parents and teachers can play in school improvement. Its usefulness for, and use by, classroom teachers to evaluate their practice will prove to be its greatest strength in an ever expanding effectiveness literature.

1999: 246 × 174mm: 176pp
Pb: 0-415-20580-8: £12.99

Published in Association with the NUT

How to Improve Your School

Tim Brighouse and David Woods

This book takes a practical look at how improvements can be made in any school

It cuts through the jargon of the specialist and shows how ideas and intentions can be turned into direct actions that will help a school improve its performance and effectiveness. As well as addressing headteachers and governors, the book will also provide invaluable guidance for all those who work in and with schools.

Current issues of debate are dealt with in a clear and informative way. There are chapters on:

- effective schools and how they have achieved their goals
- leadership within schools
- teaching and learning effectively
- making critical interventions to secure improvement
- how schools involve others to aid improvement

1999: 234 × 156mm: 192pp
Pb: 0-415-19444-X: £12.99

The Funding Revolution

New Routes to Project Fundraising

Tom Roberts

This volume looks at methods of raising funds, providing practical steps in preparing for new funding initiatives, and also focuses on the attitudes and mindsets that form part of the whole picture.

'This is a most reassuring book. It does make it all copeable by taking you by the hand, unravelling the mysteries and getting you started on the process.' – *Management in Education*

Managing Colleges Effectively

1998: 150pp
Hb: 0-7507-0822-0: £45.00
Pb: 0-7507-0821-2: £14.95